STEAM'S NEW DAWN

BRITAIN'S THIRD CENTURY OF STEAM LOCOMOTIVES

ROBIN JONES

HALSGROVE

To Jenny, Ross and Vicky

In memory of Bill Edwards (1929–2011), our family's greatest engineer

First published in Great Britain in 2011.

British Library Cataloguing-in-Publication Data
A CIP record for this title is available from the British Library

ISBN 978 0 85704 125 8

HALSGROVE
Halsgrove House,
Ryelands Industrial Estate,
Bagley Road, Wellington, Somerset TA21 9PZ
Tel: 01823 653777   Fax: 01823 216796
email: sales@halsgrove.com

Part of the Halsgrove group of companies
Information on all Halsgrove titles is available at: www.halsgrove.com

Printed and bound by Grafiche Flaminia, Italy

CONTENTS

	INTRODUCTION	5
CHAPTER ONE	**RAVENGLASS – THE FIRST NEW BUILD?**	18
CHAPTER TWO	**CONTINUING THE FAIRLIE TRADITION**	21
CHAPTER THREE	**RECREATING STEAM'S EARLY YEARS**	25
CHAPTER FOUR	**THE BROADER PICTURE**	34
CHAPTER FIVE	**THE BEATIFICATION OF A HALL**	39
CHAPTER SIX	**GWR MIX AND MATCH: A NEW GRANGE**	44
CHAPTER SEVEN	**RECREATING HAWKSWORTH'S COUNTY: THE LAST GWR 4-6-0**	50
CHAPTER EIGHT	***TORNADO* THE MAGNIFICENT!**	55
CHAPTER NINE	**A BR STANDARD 3 TANK – THE PERFECT CHOICE?**	65
CHAPTER TEN	**WHY A NORTH EASTERN G5 IS IDEAL TOO**	68
CHAPTER ELEVEN	**THE SECOND *BEACHY HEAD***	71
CHAPTER TWELVE	**BLOOMING MARVELLOUS**	74
CHAPTER THIRTEEN	**JOIN THE CLAN!**	77
CHAPTER FOURTEEN	**TENDER LOCOMOTIVE TO TANK ENGINE**	81
CHAPTER FIFTEEN	**"WE WANT OUR ENGINES BACK"**	84
CHAPTER SIXTEEN	**THE RETURN OF HUNSLET**	89
CHAPTER SEVENTEEN	***ANT* AND *BEE***	97
CHAPTER EIGHTEEN	**GWR STEAM RAILMOTOR: THE GREAT MISSING LINK**	99
CHAPTER NINETEEN	**REMEMBERING THE *UNKNOWN WARRIOR***	104
CHAPTER TWENTY	**THE RETURN OF *LEW* AND *LYN***	109
CHAPTER TWENTY ONE	**TWO NEW B17S ARE BETTER THAN ONE**	114
CHAPTER TWENTY TWO	**A NEW HOLDEN F5 TANK**	117
CHAPTER TWENTY THREE	**BRINGING BACK *BLYTH* TO SOUTHWOLD**	120
CHAPTER TWENTY FOUR	**THE GWR ENGINE THAT NEVER WAS, AND OTHER CONVERSIONS**	122
CHAPTER TWENTY FIVE	**IT'S A SMALL WORLD**	125
CHAPTER TWENTY SIX	**NEXT IN LINE**	134
CHAPTER TWENTY SEVEN	**A NEW MAIN LINE HERITAGE DIESEL?**	141
APPENDIX	**SO YOU WANT TO LIFT A SPANNER TOO?**	144

FOREWORD

I CAN WELL REMEMBER as child of only three summers standing on a station platform with my mother, being absolutely terrified of those great hissing, steaming, menacing monsters as they stopped and started just feet away from where I was standing. The shrill of the whistle made me nearly jump out of my skin and when the safety valves went off I ran behind my mother's skirts! Gradually these fears disappeared as I grew oh so slowly older and by the time I was the ripe old age of four I could stand my ground never to be terrified of steam locomotives again. Mind you the safety valves still used to make me jump when they exploded into life and they still cause a reaction even today!

It is strange how you take certain things for granted. As I grew older I would accompany my brother to watch the trains go by at the nearby level crossing. B1s, 9Fs and Britannia locomotives plus other classes that I did not know but my brother did. The school I attended was next to a railway line and more than once a shout would go out, "There's a Brit" and we all en masse would rush to the fence and eagerly search for the cab number and hope against hope that it would be a new "cop"! And then life changed; we moved to another part of the country; I made new friends, discovered music and being a teenager I did not notice the end of steam. Despite the fun and excitement it once gave me I was not there at its passing; I did not even register that it had gone. Shame on me!

Several years later I found myself immersed in the world of model planes, boats and trains and then later just trains when I joined Hornby. This gave me once more the opportunity to revive past interests and to search out steam locomotives and those people who had kept them alive. However, there was a new breed of preservationists and these hardy fellows didn't just want to find an old locomotive and rebuild it, these chaps wanted to build from scratch. One can only ponder on those intrepid men who sat in a pub nearly twenty years ago and decided that they should build a new A1; and I can only imagine how elated and overjoyed they must have been when they saw their vision take steam for the first time and move under its own power. And these intrepid pioneers are not alone. There are all manner of "new" builds in various stages of development and their perpetrators cannot help but be inspired by those magnificent "Tornado" men.

Yes the impossible can be made to be possible and this wonderful publication by Robin Jones describes how there are many new projects being undertaken by those who have a shared vision that anything *is* achievable. These men and women are making their steam dreams come true as well as bringing back fond memories to those of us who remember when steam was king and diesels were just buses on rails!

Enjoy the book – I certainly did.

Simon Kohler
Hornby

The two Hornby Railroad models of Tornado: *left is the top-of-the-range detailed model, while on the right is the less detailed version aimed for younger and less careful fans!*
ROBIN JONES

INTRODUCTION

YORK STATION WAS PACKED to overflowing on the morning of 31 January 2009. Busy throughout its history as one of the main stations on the East Coast Main Line between King's Cross and Edinburgh, the platforms were literally bursting at the seams with bystanders.

Squeezing my way through the crowds on the station footbridge, I was forced to compete not with fellow lineside photographers for the least worst position from which to take pictures through the grimy glass, but with 15-years-old girls holding mobile telephones to capture what was about to happen on video. Before this moment, they had probably never picked up a railway book or visited a heritage steam line in their lives.

The big event in this, the age of celebrities, was the birth of a new celebrity, adding to the lengthy list headed by such as David Beckham, Cheryl Cole or Robbie Williams.

This one, however, was different. It was not human, but mechanical. More than that, it was a steam railway locomotive.

For weeks leading up to the day, newspapers, TV and radio had been swooning over the prospect of a brand new full-size main line steam locomotive, shiny and gleaming out of the box just like a Hornby model wrapped in gift paper beneath the Christmas tree, running on Britain's national network, just as in the far-off days of steam.

The locomotive was A1 Pacific No. 60163 *Tornado*, the 50th member of the class designed by Arthur Henry Peppercorn, OBE (29 January 1889-3 March 1951) the last Chief Mechanical Engineer of the London & North Eastern Railway. The last of the previous 49, No. 60145 *Saint Mungo*, had been withdrawn in 1966 after a working life of just 17 years and like the rest of its sisters, sent for scrap, an attempt to preserve it for future generations having come to nothing.

STEAM'S FINAL FLINGS

Nearly half a century before, on 18 March 1960, a similar launch event took place in Swindon Works, which had been set up in 1841 by Isambard Kingdom Brunel to build locomotives for the Great Western Railway.

That day, British Railways unveiled what would be its last new steam locomotive, Standard 9F heavy freight 2-10-0 No. 92220 *Evening Star*. The British Railways Modernisation Plan of 1955 had called for the eradication of all steam haulage and its replacement with diesel and electric traction as soon as possible: however, the building of steam engines to existing orders continued for five more years to satisfy the locomotive demands of the then much-larger system.

The last express passenger locomotive built by BR had been unique Class 8P Pacific No. 71000 *Duke of Gloucester*, completed at Crewe Works in 1954.

New builds GWR steam railmotor No. 93 lines up alongside Brunswick green-liveried Peppercorn A1 Pacific No. 60163 Tornado at Didcot Railway Centre on 11 June 2011.
FRANK DUMBLETON/GWS

By the time *Evening Star* appeared, Britain, which had given the world the steam locomotive back in 1804 when Cornish mining engineer Richard Trevithick first demonstrated one in public, on the Penydarren Tramroad near Merthyr Tydfil, was somewhat late in the day in moving on to modern traction.

The final steam locomotive built for service in North America had been Norfolk & Western Railroad S1a class 0-8-0 No. 244, at Roanoke Works in December 1953. In the USSR, passenger steam locomotive building ended in 1956 with the outshopping of the final L class 2-10-0s, LV 2-10-0s and P36 4-8-4s. In Australia, the last new steam locomotive constructed was Queensland Government Railways' 3ft 6ins gauge B181/4 class 4-6-2 No 1086 in 1958.

Even private manufacturers in Britain were by then moving out of the steam market. The last Peckett locomotive was No. 2165, a 3ft gauge 0-6-0 tank engine supplied to the Sena Sugar Estates in Mozambique in 1958. Robert Stephenson & Hawthorn's was 0-6-0 fireless locomotive No. 8002, built for the National Coal Board's Glasshoughton coking plant and delivered in January 1959. The Yorkshire Engine Company's final steam locomotive was a pannier tank, No. 2584, built for the Western Region in 1956. Sentinel, famous for its vertical-boilered industrial locomotive, turned out its last steam engine the following year.

Evening Star, however, was not the last steam locomotive built in Britain for commercial, as opposed to tourist or leisure, purposes.

It was in 1963 that the last order for two steam locomotives for British use was delivered by a home-based manufacturer. Standard gauge Hunslet Austerity 0-6-0 saddle tanks Nos, 3889 and 3890 were finished on 18 March and 23 March respectively. Although the pair were built for industrial use, arguably they were main line types as many of the earlier Austerity 0-6-0STs built during World War Two were later taken into main line service as the LNER J94 class. Austerity 0-6-0STs had been the

The most recent express passenger steam locomotives built in Britain: Tornado, *carrying its first livery of British Railways apple green, lines up alongside broad gauge* Fire Fly *at Didcot Railway Centre.* FRANK DUMBLETON/GWS

Sean Bolan's painting of GWR steam railmotor No. 93 alongside new GWR Saint No. 2999 Lady of Legend *at Henley-in-Arden station in Warwickshire.*

standard British shunting locomotive during World War Two, and were also built to a Hunslet design by several other manufacturers. Both engines were sold for £15,000 each. No. 3889 was sent to Manvers Coal Preparation Plant and No. 3890 to Cadeby Main Colliery, Conisborough, where it became No. 66 in the South Yorkshire NCB fleet. When the Conisborough area was designated a smokeless zone in 1970, the locomotive, the 484th Austerity saddle tank to be built, was replaced by an ex-British Rail diesel shunter. No. 3890, which is therefore of tremendous historical significance, was in the autumn of 1975 bought for preservation at the Buckinghamshire Railway Centre. At the time of writing, a major overhaul to return it to steam for the first time in the heritage era was making progress.

Andrew Barclay built its last steam locomotive, 0-6-2 works No. 2377, for export to Indonesia in September 1962, the order having been transferred from Stafford manufacturer WG Bagnall & Co which had ceased building.

Hudswell Clarke's last steam locomotive was 0-4-0 saddle tank No. 1893, supplied to the National Coal Board in 1961.

Steam building at the Leeds firm of Hunslet, however, lingered on for a few more years. In 1962, Hunslet carried out the almost complete rebuilding of the Snowdon Mountain Railway's SLM, 1896-built 0-4-2T No 4 *Snowdon*, which had lain derelict at Llanberis for many years. Only the frame plates and one cylinder from the original locomotive saw service again, and therefore it might technically be considered to be a Hunslet 'new build', although convention has it that the identity of a locomotive is taken from its frames.

In 1967, Hunslet collaborated in the building of a new batch of 2ft gauge NGG16 articulated Beyer Garratts for South African Railways, and supplied eight boilers to Hunslet Taylor Consolidated in Johannesburg.

While the steam age might be considered to have begun with the building of a little-known Trevithick at Coalbrookdale Ironworks in 1802, it ended in 1971, when Hunslet outshopped its last steam locomotive at Leeds.

The first locomotive exported by Hunslet went to Java in 1866. Ironically, it was the last steam age engine built in Britain, by Hunslet, that went to the same island. It was 0-4-2ST No. 3902, which was largely assembled by parts that had been in store for many years. Built to the Kerr Stuart Brazil class design of 2ft/2ft 6in gauge locomotives which Hunslet had inherited when it acquired the assets of that company, it became No. 4 in the Trangkil sugar plantation fleet, and worked for 33 years before becoming redundant by rationalisation of the estate's railway system.

There was no 'farewell fanfare' of the kind that was laid on for the launch of *Evening Star*, as No. 3902 was quietly shipped out abroad. More of Trangkil No. 4 later.

THE BEGINNINGS OF RAILWAY HERITAGE

The dates of 1802, 1804, 1960 and 1971 for that matter, are seminal to the history of the steam locomotive, as is 1825, when the world's first steam-powered public railway, the Stockton & Darlington opened, and 1829, when George Stephenson's Rocket won the Rainhill Trials.

A lesser-known date in the story is 1836. That is the date when railway preservation began, when *Invicta*, built by Robert Stephenson & Company immediately after *Rocket*, was withdrawn from service on the Canterbury & Whitstable Railway. Offered for sale, there were no takers but rather than being scrapped, a fate which had quickly befallen the Trevithick pioneer locomotives, it was placed in storage, and eventually passed into the ownership of the South Eastern Railway. It has become the first railway locomotive to be saved for posterity.

BR Standard 9F 2-10-0 No. 92220 Evening Star, *which in 1960 was the last steam locomotive built for main line use in Britain, before the debut of A1 Peppercorn Pacific No. 60163* Tornado *on the national network in 2009.* NRM

Displayed at the Golden Jubilee of the Stockton & Darlington Railway in 1875 and at the Newcastle Stephenson Centenary in 1881, restoration began in 1892. At one stage, *Invicta*, painted bright red, was displayed in Canterbury's Dane John Gardens. A full cosmetic restoration began in

1977, in time for *Invicta* to take part in the 150th anniversary of the Canterbury & Whitstable Railway on 3 May 1980. It is currently one of the star exhibits inside Canterbury Museum.

Many, many more locomotives would follow in *Invicta's* wake – as the opportunities for preservation arose.

In some cases, railway companies would set aside locomotives to be mounted for display. In other cases, redundant engines might be acquired by museums.

However, while *Rocket* ended up as a Science Museum exhibit, there was no guarantee that every locomotive which represented a landmark in the evolution of the steam engine, or was the last survivor of a major class of engines, would be preserved. Indeed, in most cases it did not happen. Therefore, if you look at today's collection of heritage locomotives as a whole and try to outline the story of the development of the steam engine from the 1802 Coalbrookdale locomotive onwards, there will inevitably be huge gaps.

In 1951, the British Transport Commission began moves to consolidate attempts by the pre-nationalisation railway companies in preserving locomotives, and eventually authorised the compilation of an official list of those which were to be publicly preserved. When they were taken out of traffic, rather than being sent straight to the scrapyard, the earmarked engines were stored in sheds and works throughout the country, while others were placed on loan to local authority museums. The items officially set aside for preservation became known as the National Collection.

The move, though laudable, would never please anyone. There was never any intention to save an example of every single type of locomotive, but to focus on examples which highlighted a particular stage of development of the steam engine. For most enthusiasts, however, there were glaring examples: the world's most famous steam locomotive, LNER A3 Pacific No. 4472 *Flying Scotsman*, was omitted, along with every other member of the class: had it not been for Ffestiniog saviour Alan Pegler buying it in 1963, it could well have been turned into razor blades and sardine tins. Thankfully it was saved, and after being bought by the National Railway Museum in 2004 for £2.31-million, it is now part of the National Collection. Many other classic locomotives, however, were not that fortunate.

Another key year is 1951. It was in spring that year that a group of West Midlands-based volunteers under the leadership of transport historian Tom Rot began running the closure-threatened Talyllyn Railway, a private 2ft 3in gauge line in central Wales.

The Talyllyn became the first railway in the world to be saved and operated by volunteers, and kickstarted today's operational heritage railway movement. It was followed by the Ffestiniog Railway revival, the saving of the Welshpool & Llanfair Light Railway, the opening of the first section of the Bluebell Railway, the Keighley & Worth Valley Railway and many more. Today there are well over 100 operational steam railways in the British Isles, and they form a significant slice of the tourist market.

This book does not propose to document the magnificent achievements of the heritage railway sector, for that would be a sizeable volume in itself, but suffice it to say that the dauntless efforts of an army of more than 20,000 volunteers across the country have forced the word 'impossible' to be

Opposite: *The last express passenger steam locomotive built for use on the British national network before* Tornado *was unique 8P Pacific No. 71000 Duke of Gloucester in 1954. However, it realised its true potential only after it was preserved despite being partially cut up – one of many heritage era miracles that showed that building new main line locomotives was possible. It is seen heading the Railway Touring Company's 'Great Britain' through Magor in South Wales in April 2007.* BRIAN SHARPE

redefined. They have literally moved mountains. When, for instance, the Ffestiniog revivalists found that the Central Electricity Generating Board had been given the go-ahead to flood part of its line with the Llyn Ystradau hydro-electric plant reservoir, they set to work and chiselled a bypass route along the adjoining hillside, creating a spiral loop that is more akin to Indian lines like the Darjeeling Himalayan Railway than anything else in Britain.

British Railway's final steam design, *Duke of Gloucester*, lasted only eight years in service. A prototype of what had been intended to be a much larger class, it incorporated three sets of modified Caprotti valve gear, relatively new to British locomotive engineering and more efficient than Walschaerts or Stephenson valve gear.

However, No. 71000 was regarded as a failure by locomotive crews due to its poor steaming characteristics and its heavy fuel consumption. There was also problems with poor draughting of the locomotive which led to it failing to keep to timetables.

When the Modernisation Plan was announced only a year after *Duke of Gloucester* appeared, it was decided not to go ahead with modifications which would have made its design far more successful. No. 71000 lasted in service only for eight years, and was withdrawn in 1962.

It was initially selected for the National Collection, but the experts who compiled the list subsequently decided that only the cylinder arrangement was of historical interest. One of the Duke's outside cylinders was removed for display at the Science Museum, while the locomotive was then sold for scrap, to one Dai Woodham, whose breaker's yard was based at Barry in South Wales.

Dai Woodham is a seminal figure in our story. In 1958, his firm Woodham Brothers won a tender to scrap British Railways locomotives, wagons and rail, and on 25 March 1959, the first batch of engines was sent from Swindon to Barry.

By 1965, Dai had reached the conclusion that scrapping wagons was more profitable than cutting up steam locomotives, which were shunted aside for a rainy day. While other scrapyards elsewhere in Britain reduced locomotives to a pile of scrap metal often within days of their arrival, rows and rows of mainly Great Western and Southern Railway types rusted away in the Bristol Channel air.

Dai's decision led to 213 locomotives being bought for the rapidly-growing railway preservation movement before his scrapyard closed in the late eighties. Indeed, the availability of such a large number of engines may be regarded as a backbone of the heritage sector.

However, while GWR and Southern types were often represented many times over, there was no benevolent scrapman in LMS or LNER territory, and so numerous classic locomotive types were rendered extinct because the preservation movement had not gathered sufficient strength to save them.

Duke of Gloucester minus its cylinder also languished in the scrapyard. Over the years, revivalists often came to view the locomotives at Woodham Brothers, cherry picking the best for restoration and a second life on their heritage lines. However, nobody took the restoration of No. 71000 seriously, until a group of enthusiasts pushed the boat out and daringly bought the locomotive in 1974, forming the Duke of Gloucester Steam Locomotive Trust.

It took 13 years to restore 'the one that couldn't be done' to working order. During the restoration, however, the restorers made several discoveries regarding flaws in the original design. Firstly, the chimney was too small compared with other locomotives of similar size, resulting in poor boiler draughting at times of high steam demand.

Furthermore, the grate air inlet dampers had not been built in accordance with the drawings, and were too small, resulting in poor air supply and inefficient combustion.

Those rebuilding the scrap locomotive not only corrected both inadequacies, but made other improvements, including the Kylchap exhaust system that had been recommended by British Railways engineers, but never installed.

The net result was then when it ran again, *Duke of Gloucester's* failings had been addressed, and it could finally demonstrate its true potential as a powerful express passenger locomotive.

Not only had the trust restored No. 71000, but had in effect implemented the modifications which should have been made by British Railways. Therefore Britain's last main line steam design showed its true capabilities only in the preservation era!

As the volunteer-led railway preservation movement snowballed in the seventies and eighties, with more lines being opened and extended, and locomotives and rolling stock restored, the question inevitably arose – if we can hone 'hopeless' engines like *Duke of Gloucester* to perfection, could we not go on to build new ones, and fill in those missing gaps?

FROM LITTLE ACORNS…

Building locomotives for tourist and leisure purposes was nothing new. You only have to look at the plethora of seaside miniature railways that were flourishing in many British resorts during the early and mid-twentieth century, not to mention the countless number of small-scale private railways.

These had their beginnings in the work of Sir Arthur Percival Heywood, 3rd Baronet, (25 December1849-19 April 1916) who built a 4in gauge model railway with a steam locomotive as a teenager. However, he wanted something that his younger brothers could ride on, and so constructed a 9in gauge line as well, only to find that it was too unstable to carry passengers properly.

After his marriage in 1872 he set up home at Duffield Bank in Derbyshire and mixed with many Midland Railway directors who lived locally. Following on from experiments by the Royal Engineers to produce narrow gauge railways which could be used in battlefield situations, he built a 15in gauge line on his land, as a prototype in the hope of selling the concept to others. His first locomotive there was an 0-4-0 named *Effie*.

Known as the Duffield Bank Railway, it attracted much interest, but the only person who commissioned him to build

The last 'steam age' locomotive built in Britain, Hunslet 0-4-2ST Trangkil No. 4, outshopped in 1971 and now running on the 1½-mile dual gauge line at the Statfold Barn Railway. ROBIN JONES

In September 2010, the first of six driving wheels for the new LMS Patriot 4-6-0 No. 45551 The Unknown Warrior *were cast at Boro Foundry of Lye, West Midlands, after readers of* Heritage Railway *magazine raised £60,000 in a nationwide appeal. The author and magazine editor is pictured alongside.*
ROBIN JONES

one was the Duke of Westminster, at his Eaton Hall seat in Cheshire.

The subsequent 15in gauge Eaton Hall Railway ran three miles to the GWR station sidings at Balderton on the Shrewsbury to Chester line, with a maximum gradient of 1-in-70. A branch line served the estate's brickyard.

Three engines were supplied, the first an 0-4-0T named *Katie* followed by two identical 0-6-0Ts named *Shelagh* and *Ursula*.

The duke's railway paved the way for hundreds of miniature railways and locomotives and carriages to run on them to be built in the twentieth century, including the Romney, Hythe & Dymchurch Railway in Kent, the Fairbourne Railway in central Wales and the Ravenglass & Eskdale Railway in the Lake District.

While British manufacturers ceased full-size steam locomotive production in the fifties and sixties, the technology never went away. Model engineers continued to build miniature steam engines in their private sheds, garages and private workshops, and many societies were formed with their own dedicated running lines. Also, several firms continued building miniature steam locomotives for amusement lines.

In the twenty-first century, market-leading model manufacturer Hornby even produced OO gauge locomotives which could run on steam, rather than be driven by an electric motor hidden inside a steam outline body, as per the model railway norm.

Yet while steam building never died out, building a new full-size locomotive would of course be an entirely different matter. This book looks at how we got from the hobbyist's lathe and toolset to *Tornado* and the main line – and the other new build projects that have either been completed or are underway.

WHAT IS 'NEW BUILD'?

The primary reason why a group of individuals would want to build a new steam locomotive is the desire to fill a gap in today's heritage locomotive fleet, bringing a much-loved locomotive type, an example of which should have been saved but wasn't, back to life.

Then there are those who commission miniature or narrow gauge locomotives for use at tourist attractions or other private railways. These can be replicas of originals, maybe scaled down to a quarter size, or freelance designs.

The term 'new build' in its purest form literally means building a locomotive from scratch – constructing every part from new. This is basically the case with *Tornado*.

Then there are those projects which are based on recycling components from other locomotives to recreate extinct ones.

Such schemes are largely possible through the policy of GWR Chief Mechanical Engineer George Jackson Churchward who developed a series of standard locomotives, with many parts such as wheels, cylinders and connecting rods being interchangeable between different classes. Therefore the situation arose whereby if you have several examples of a particular GWR type in preservation, but none of another, it is possible to fill the void by using components from unrestored examples of abundantly-represented classes while building some new parts. This method, which mainly draws on locomotives saved from Barry scrapyard, is somewhat of a 'halfway house' scheme when compared to the likes of *Tornado*.

In some cases, 'new' locomotives can be created simply by converting one type into another. Such conversions can be carried out at a minimalist level, such as repainting an example of the abovementioned Hunslet Austerity saddle tanks into a livery matching the LNER or British Railways colours that other examples carried, thereby turning an industrial locomotive with esoteric appeal into a main line type which may instigate wider interest. Such repaints allow heritage railways with smaller locomotive fleets to run 'genuine' British Railways trains rather than one hauled non-authentically by an industrial type.

What concerns us in this book, however, are the projects in which a locomotive has been physically altered to resemble another, such as the conversion of a tank engine into a tender engine and vice versa. In the strictest sense of the word, that is also creating a 'new' locomotive, albeit at the expense of an existing one.

SO YOU WANT TO BUILD A NEW LOCOMOTIVE?

Just as it is easy for a railway enthusiast to browse Ordnance Survey maps and dream up a case of why a particular closed route should be rebuilt, so there are those whose heart's desire is to recreate a favourite locomotive that they remember from the steam era, or which is deemed to have great historical worth, and which no longer exists.

It is very easy for a handful of like-minded steam buffs to draw up such schemes on the back of a beermat, before setting up a website and writing to the enthusiast railway press announcing their official launch.

Despite the abundance of new build projects at the time of writing, August 2011, that is the first and last of the easy parts. Wishful thinking is one thing – but even seriously considering the practicality of building a particular locomotive is another.

Firstly, the question as to whether engineering drawings still exist has to be addressed. The National Railway Museum is an excellent place to start, but it is by no means guaranteed that original drawings still exist. If they do not, producing replacements is likely to be a costly and time-consuming exercise that might not necessarily be accurate.

Once the drawings are prepared, plans have to be made for producing individual components large and small, from the boilers down to the hornguides. What suppliers are available, and do they have the capacity to produce such parts to the standard required? Of course, many smaller components can be produced by a skilled engineer in a heritage railway's workshop or even a household garage, but others will require specialists to make

Early and late periods of steam locomotive development: On 4 February 2010, Tornado *visited the Museum of Science & Industry in Manchester, hauling the Royal Train carrying Prince Charles, and came face to face with the new-build Liverpool & Manchester Railway* Planet.
ROBIN JONES

15

patterns and cast and machine them.

A big short cut is to investigate commonality with other locomotives for availability of patterns and spares. In addition to locomotives which conform to the GWR standardisation policy, other companies' engines may have many similarities to sister or predecessor types. Again, this can help when drawings for certain parts are absent.

What also should be considered from the outset is certification, not only of the boiler – essential if the locomotive is to be allowed to operate – but also for main line running. Insurance companies and a locomotive's Vehicle Acceptance Body will want to see that every part has passed the British Standards test, and it is intended to run the locomotive on the national network rather than just on 25mph heritage railways, the level of inspection has to be much higher and far more expensive.

At this stage, a prospective new-build group needs to carefully assess exactly what resources are required to turn their dream into reality. It has to be remembered that in the days of steam, railway companies had purpose-built locomotive works, and could build a new engine within weeks, but today, components must be sourced from a variety of suppliers.

Colin Wright's limited edition fundraising print of new-build LMS Patriot No. 45551 The Unknown Warrior *on shed at Llangollen.*
LMS-PATRIOT PROJECT

Enthusiasts come with an abundance of knowledge and passion, but what is far more important is the raising of finance. Without it, a project cannot succeed, or will give the impression it is dragging on endlessly and lose support if supporters come to believe they will not see the locomotive run in their lifetimes.

However, miniature and some narrow gauge locomotives apart, there has been no case where the whole finance immediately becomes available.

The likely overall cost and duration of a project has to be worked out.

Sponsors need to be sought – would a particular firm be prepared to produce castings, for example, at cost price in return for publicity?

All fundraising options need to be explored, whether it is collecting old newspapers for pulping, shaking cans, selling souvenirs, a share issue, bank loans or hosting crowd-pulling events on a particular railway, with the profits going to the scheme in question. Experience has shown that multiple income streams need to be pursued with vigour. Mark Allatt, chairman of The A1 Steam Locomotive Trust which took 18 years to build *Tornado*, insists with total justification that this is the key area in which projects fail or succeed.

Several new-build groups found early on that the Heritage Lottery Fund, a major benefactor to the preservation sector, will not award grant aid to projects that aim to recreate a particular locomotive, as opposed to restoring an existing artefact. A demarcation line had to be set and this is it, again underlining the difficulty in obtaining large amounts of money fairly quickly.

Once the locomotive is ready, it will attract hire fees from the railway or main line operators who wish to run it. Can these be used to finance loans taken out to fund its construction?

The more support a group can gather, and the more new members it can recruit, the more the likelihood of success.

Therefore, when choosing which extinct locomotive to replicate, the question has to be asked –

how many people are interested in seeing one run again?

Peppercorn's A1s were remembered with much affection, and The A1 Steam Locomotive Trust was able to recruit hundreds of covenantors, supporters who agreed to pay a set sum each month by standing order, from a few pounds upwards. That guaranteed a steady income stream and as the project gathered credibility, new supporters came on board and added their weight from their wallets.

Locomotive types have to appeal to sponsors and also the railway press. If a group containing several known experts announced, for instance, it was setting out to build a replica of Britain's first Pacific, GWR No. 111 *The Great Bear*, it would be likely to be front cover news on a railway magazine. By comparison, if a less well-known group announces plans to build a little-known locomotive type from, say, the early twentieth century, which never made the headlines and nobody alive today recalls, and which will be used on a purely local basis, the story is likely to be given less prominence, in theory instigating less interest and less funds.

A locomotive has also to be attractive to operators. A tank engine may secure a contract to run on a heritage railway, but would it be powerful to justifying certification for main line running – and if so, which operators if any would be interested in hiring it? Would it be sufficiently powerful to haul a train of a required length to ensure a profit? While passengers have flocked to ride behind *Tornado*, would an example of a class with a far lower stature have the same wow appeal to the general public as opposed to the enthusiast market?

There are those who ask why bother to build new when there are so many historic locomotives that are either waiting for overhaul or yet to be restored. On the other hand, a new locomotive should, in theory at least, gives many years of service in regular use on short heritage railways or occasional main line trips without the need for major overhauls and repairs. With the decline in the number of regular volunteers that has been experienced by several heritage railways in recent years, how many restoration projects yet to be started will still happen? Would it not be easier to take out commercial loans to complete a new-build project which would require less maintenance and volunteer input?

At this point, the question has to be asked – what is the ideal size of locomotive for the average heritage railway? Once identified, could a batch be built, bringing down the overall cost of each?

As a long-time supporter of new-build projects, I believe that the answer may well lie in the Severn Valley Railway-based scheme to recreate a British Railways Standard 3MT 2-6-2 tank engine, the last examples of which were rendered extinct by the scrapman in 1968. Of a far more modest size than *Tornado*, proponents claim with much justification that it is the 'right' size for operating on a railway of about 8 to 10 miles each way, and would also be historically appropriate to many areas of Britain.

Despite main line steam haulage having ended on British Railways more than four decades ago, heritage railways seem more popular than ever, with many regularly breaking passenger records.

In some cases, the replacement of worn parts on historic engines will mean that, like today's *Flying Scotsman*, precious little of the as-built original is left. It may well be that for the bigger lines at least, new build will be part of the long-term future.

This replica of Sir Arthur Percival Heywood's pioneer 15in gauge 0-4-0 Effie *was built by Great Northern Steam of Darlington in 1999 and is part of the Cleethorpes Coast Light Railway collection. Another Heywood replica, that of 0-4-0* Ursula *built for the Eaton Hall Railway, and built by enthusiast James Waterfield, runs on the Perrygrove Railway in the Forest of Dean.* ROBIN JONES

The modern replica of Ursula *at Eaton Hall in 2002; the driver is Sir Peter Heywood, none other than the great grandson of Sir Arthur Heywood, assisted by Peter van Zeller from the Ravenglass & Eskdale Railway.* MICHAEL CROFTS

CHAPTER ONE
RAVENGLASS – THE FIRST NEW BUILD?

IT IS A MATTER OF OPINION as to which steam locomotive was the 'first' new build, that is, a steam locomotive built for historical, educational, tourist or leisure purposes as opposed to traditional commercial uses, such as service on the national network or on industrial lines. As we have seen, the building of new locomotives for miniature railways has been carrying on since the Heywood era of the 1860s.

For me, the parameter must be to limit the subject to locomotives built in the heritage era for heritage or leisure purposes.

In that case, a prime contender must be the Ravenglass & Eskdale Railway Preservation Society's 2-8-2 *River Mite*.

Northern Rock, *built at Ravenglass in 1976, with Scafell Pike, England's highest mountain, in the distance.* RER

Full steam ahead for River Mite, *arguably the heritage era's first new-build locomotive for a passenger-carrying public railway.* RER

This classic 15in gauge line, of one Britain's most popular heritage railways, started out as a 3ft gauge concern laid to transport haematite iron ore from Lakeland mines to the Furness Railway's standard gauge main line at Ravenglass and opened on 24 May 1875. The first public narrow-gauge railway in England, passengers were carried from 1876 until November 1908. The line closed in April 1913 after demand for iron ore fell while summer passenger levels dropped off.

In 1915, model railway manufacturers Wenman Joseph Bassett-Lowke and Robert Proctor-Mitchell, bought the line and halved the gauge, introducing miniature versions of main line locomotive types. Some of the rolling stock came from Sir Arthur Heywood's Duffield Bank line following his death in 1916.

The Ravenglass line reopened on 28 August 1915, with part of the railway running as dual gauge, with rails laid to accommodate standard gauge with the miniature line running between. The miniature line served tourists, while the standard gauge railway transported granite.

After World War Two, the line was bought by the Keswick Granite Company, whose quarries closed in 1953. Eventually, the company offered the railway for sale, and announced that 1960 would be the last season of passenger traffic.

Local people joined forces with enthusiasts to form the preservation society to save the line, but could not raise sufficient money. Midland stockbroker Colin Gilbert and local landowner Sir Wavell Wakefield stepped in on the day of the auction and paid the balance of the purchase price.

The society's task was to return the railway to profitability, and after a few years, it became clear that another locomotive was needed. The answer was *River Mite*, which was commissioned from builder Clarkson of York.

The locomotive part was all new, but the old eight-wheeled steam tender from 1923-built Davey Paxman 2-8-2 *River Esk* was used. The two locomotives look very similar, apart from fine details such as the cab and running boards.

It has a miniature main line outline styled on an LNER Gresley P1 2-8-2 locomotive and an LMS Stanier tender. It cost around £8,000, raised entirely by voluntary subscription as are all the major maintenance costs today.

Fundraising for the building of the new locomotive began in 1963. It was delivered in December 1966 hauled from York to Ravenglass by traction engine Providence, and commissioned on 20 May 1967.

River Mite gave the railway the capacity to operate a longer and more intensive summer service. It now carries the Furness Railway's distinctive Indian red livery.

The railway then built a new steam locomotive by itself.

After taking the Romney, Hythe & Dymchurch Railway's Davey Paxman 4-6-2 No. 2 *Northern Chief* on trial in 1972, it was decided to construct a new 2-6-2, originally intended to be named *Sir Arthur Heywood* in honour of the great miniature railway pioneer.

However, the railway received funding from the Northern Rock building society (subsequently a bank) and so the locomotive was named after its main sponsor.

The locomotive was built in the railway's own workshops at Ravenglass. It entered traffic in 1976 and has since visited many railways, as far afield as Dresden in Germany, to publicise the Ravenglass & Eskdale.

It was so successful that two similar locomotives were built at Ravenglass for Japan's Shuzenji Romney Railway, *Northern Rock II* in 1989 and *Cumbria* in 1992, respectively.

Northern Rock carries Highland Railway muscat green livery with red and dark green lining. Despite the bank being taken into state ownership during the credit crisis in 2007, the name has stayed.

Locomotive building at Ravenglass continued with the building of two diesels, Bo-Bo *Lady Wakefield* in 1980 and in 2005 Bo-Bo *Douglas Ferreira*, after the general manager of the railway from 1961 to 1994.

In the new-build scheme of things, 1979 is a seminal date. That was when the Ffestiniog Railway completed a seven-year project to build a new double Fairlie locomotive, *Earl of Merioneth*.

CHAPTER TWO
CONTINUING THE FAIRLIE TRADITION

THREE ASPECTS OF THIS PROJECT set it apart from many of the new-builds that followed over the next third of a century. Firstly, it was built under the Fairlie patent... which the Ffestiniog has a licence in perpetuity to use.

Secondly, it was built at the line's Boston Lodge Works, where double Fairlies and a single one too had been built decades before the preservation era.

Thirdly, it was not a replica of a previous double Fairlie, but built to a modern design of the concept, with sloping square tanks.

While it might be argued that the Ravenglass & Eskdale locomotives are a 'halfway' house between miniature railways and narrow gauge, at least in terms of appearance, there is no doubting that Earl of Merioneth is a full-size locomotive, built for regular haulage of passenger trains on a public railway rather than short rides on a demonstration line or occasional loan visits, and therefore may be considered the first of its kind in the heritage movement.

Victorian engineer, Robert Francis Fairlie came up with a simple answer to the problem of having to turn an engine when it reaches its destination – build one with two ends. The cabs are joined back

The building of Earl of Merioneth *began in 1972, a century after the Ffestiniog Railway outshopped its first double Fairlie at Boston Lodge Works. It is seen entering Porthmadog Harbour station in 2011.* ANDREW THOMAS/FR

21

to back to make one, and there were two articulated power bogies.

The double Fairlies, one of the trademarks of the Ffestiniog, might look eccentric by the standard of conventional locomotives, but Fairlie was far sighted: most modern main line diesel locomotives have cabs at either end.

It was *Little Wonder*, built by George England to Fairlie's design in 1869 for the 11ft 11½in gauge Ffestiniog, which brought Fairlie international fame and fortune.

On 11 February 1870, Fairlie hosted locomotive engineers as far afield as Russia, Mexico, Turkey and Sweden at the Ffestiniog where he ran *Little Wonder*. Orders for the new type of locomotive poured in, and Fairlie was so pleased that he gave the Festiniog Railway Company a permanent licence to use his locomotive patent without restriction in return for using the line to demonstrate *Little Wonder*, which was successful in that it could travel around the line's tight curves at a respectable speed, meaning that the expensive previous plans to double the track were rendered redundant.

By 1876, 43 different railways around the world had operated his engines, but apart from Mexico, New Zealand and on the Ffestiniog, it did not last. There were reports of dissatisfaction with the limited capacity for fuel and water, the flexible steam pipes being prone to leakage and wasting of power and the absence of unpowered wheels, which on traditional steam engines act as stabilisers.

For customers too cautious to try a double-ended locomotive, Fairlie built 'single' versions, a double Fairlie cut in half.

Little Wonder was scrapped in 1882. A second double Fairlie, No. 8 *James Spooner* of 1889, lasted until 1933 when it met the same fate.

The line's third double Fairlie, No. 10 *Merddin Emrys*, was built at the line's own Boston Lodge Works in 1872 and is still in service today. No. 11 *Livingston Thompson* was built there in 1886.

While volunteers were hacking their way through slate country with the reservoir deviation, Ffestiniog officials were looking forward to the time when their trains would again run into Blaenau Ffestiniog. More motive power was needed, and what better than to build a traditional Ffestiniog 0-4-0+0-4-0T design at Boston Lodge. It was also built to replace *Livingston Thompson*, which is now on static display at the National Railway Museum in York.

Building work began in 1972 following delivery of the boiler. Designed like the original Fairlies for coal burning, oil tanks and oil burning equipment

Opposite: Named after the Liberal Prime Minister, a local solicitor who regularly travelled on the railway, David Lloyd George carries its name in English on one side and the Welsh Defied Lloyd George on the other side. FR

The Ffestiniog Railway's new-build single Fairlie Taliesin incorporates a few parts of its predecessor. FR

Back in 1869, Little Wonder *was the Festiniog (then spelled with one f) Railway's first double Fairlie and its demonstration made its designer a fortune.* FR

were fitted in 1978 before the boiler was first steamed. It was converted to coal firing in 2007, due to the by-then significant difference in the prices of oil and coal. Despite its modern appearance, *Earl of Merioneth* was so successful that in 1992, Boston Lodge outshopped another, No. 12 David Lloyd George, which was built over three years to a more conventional rounded shape.

Originally the proposal here was just to build a new boiler for *Earl of Merioneth* – but the project got carried away with itself to the point where a new locomotive appeared.

Because the boiler is designed to operate at a higher pressure and has a greater degree of superheat than any other double Fairlie example, *David Lloyd George* is the most powerful steam locomotive ever to run in normal service on the Ffestiniog, able to haul 12 coaches efficiently and economically.

The Ffestiniog also owned and operated *Taliesin*, a single Fairlie 0-4-4T built by Vulcan Foundry, from 1876 to 1927. It was scrapped in 1935 after no money could be found for a new boiler, but a replica was built at Boston Lodge between 1996-99, the new *Taliesin* first steaming on 11 April that year. After further modifications it entered public passenger service in late August 2000.

Incorporating a few parts surviving from the original, some supports claimed that *Taliesin* is not a new-build but a 'heavy general overhaul' of the first one!

CHAPTER THREE
RECREATING STEAM'S EARLY YEARS

BEFORE *INVICTA* WAS SET ASIDE, no thought appears to have been given to preserving pioneer railway locomotives.

Once the idea of using steam locomotives rather than horses took off in the coalfields of the north east, the evolution of their design was reasonably rapid, each new one learning from the flaws of its predecessor. Consequently, several of the early locomotives were rendered obsolete very quickly and met the only fate available at the time.

Britain reshaped the world through the invention of the steam locomotive. It was to have a far more profound impact on the globe than its empire, which it helped facilitate.

Therefore, it was a logical step for those involved in railway heritage and history to want to bring pioneer locomotives from the dawn of steam back to life.

Furthermore, these early locomotives were comparatively simple affairs, and on cost alone lent themselves to early new-build projects.

In 1975, Beamish Museum in County Durham, arguably the world leader in the study of early steam railways, built a working replica of *Locomotion No. 1*, the first locomotive to run on the Stockton & Darlington Railway, the world's first public steam railway, which opened on 27 September 1825. It was then that the first steam-hauled public passenger train ran and carried up to 600 passengers, most sitting in empty coal wagons and a select few in a passenger coach called the Experiment.

Built in George and Robert Stephenson's works under Timothy Hackworth, the design of *Locomotion No. 1* involved high-pressure steam from a centre-flue boiler driving two vertical cylinders, from which a pair of yokes transmitted the power downwards, through pairs of connecting rods, to the wheels. It was one of the first locomotives to use coupling rods rather than chains or gears to link its 0-4-0 wheel arrangement together. Incidentally, the scheduled passenger trains on the Stockton & Darlington for some years after its

The 'twice-built' replica of Rocket, *seen at an open weekend at Tyseley Locomotive Works in June 2011.* ROBIN JONES

The National Railway Museum's 'cutaway' replica of Rocket *and two Liverpool & Manchester Railway carriages.* ROBIN JONES

The 1989 replica of Trevithick's Coalbrookdale engine of 1802.

illustrious opening were horse-drawn affairs.

With later advances in design, *Locomotion No. 1* quickly became obsolete. Withdrawn from service in 1841, it was turned into a stationary engine, but in 1857, it was preserved. It is now on display at the Darlington's Head of Steam railway museum at North Road station and is part of the National Collection.

While to return an artefact of immense historical importance like the original *Locomotion No. 1* to working order was unthinkable, the Beamish replica, first steamed in public 150 years after the original was unveiled, regularly runs on the museum's standard gauge Pockerley Waggonway.

In 1980, the Rocket 150 event remembering the Rainhill Trials of 1829 won by George Stephenson's locomotive of the same name was staged by the Liverpool & Manchester Railway, to choose the best form of traction.

Especially for the occasion, a working replica of one of the entrants, John Ericsson and John Braithwaite's 0-2-2 well tank *Novelty*, which has been hailed as the world's first tank engine, was built by Locomotive Enterprises at the preserved Bowes Railway in County Durham.

In 1982, it was sold to the Swedish Railway Museum in Gävle. Another version on static display in the Museum of Science & Industry in Manchester includes parts from the original and dates from 1929.

Also unveiled in April 1980 when it steamed for the first time was a replica of another Rainhill Trials entrant, Timothy Hackworth's *Sans Pareil*. It had been built the year before by apprentices at British Rail Engineering Ltd's Shildon workshops and then took part in the Rocket 150 celebration cavalcade at Rainhill.

Both the original locomotive and the replica have been on display at Locomotion: The National Railway Museum at Shildon since the museum opened in 2004.

In 2009, the museum's conservation workshop cosmetically restored the replica, and as a result of research by early railways expert Jim Rees, it was repainted in the colours carried by the original. The following year, the replica visited the Nuremberg Transport Museum as part of special events to celebrate the 175th anniversary of the first steam locomotive trip in Germany.

Of course, the most famous early locomotive of all has to be *Rocket* itself. The 0-2-2 transformed steam haulage by combining the technologies of blastpipes and multi-tube boilers, thereby producing a locomotive powerful enough to haul passenger trains on the world's first inter-city railway.

Not surprisingly, several replicas have been built over the years, while what is left of the original is displayed in the Science Museum.

A full-size replica of *Rocket* was depicted on a London & North Western Railway postcard sometime before 1923, but little more appears to be known about it. A working replica was built in 1923 for the Buster Keaton silent movie *Our Hospitality*, and also appeared in the film *The Iron Mule* two years later. It has now disappeared into obscurity.

Robert Stephenson & Hawthorns in 1929 supplied one to the Henry Ford Museum in Detroit.

An impressive cutaway static replica constructed in 1935 and displayed alongside the original in the Science Museum is now in the Great Hall at the National Railway Museum, along with a pair of replica Liverpool & Manchester carriages.

Incidentally, also built in 1935 was a working replica of *Der Adler*, a 2-2-2 built in 1835 by the Stephensons for the Bavarian Ludwigsbahn between Nuremberg and Fürth and scrapped in 1857. The replica is now in the Deutsche Bahn museum in Nuremberg.

In 1979, a magnificent working replica of *Rocket* was built by engineer Mike Satow and his Locomotion Enterprises for the Rocket 150 anniversary celebrations at Rainhill. First of all, however, it was displayed in Kensington Gardens, London, on the 150th anniversary of the trials.

A frequent visitor to heritage railways, it was fitted with a

The 1981-built replica of Trevithick's Penydarren locomotive at Railfest 2004. ROBIN JONES

chimney shorter than the original in order to the clear the bridge at Rainhill, as there is now less headroom than when the line was built in the 1820s.

Both of these replicas are now based at the National Railway Museum.

The 1979 *Rocket* also has the unique claim to having been built new twice. In 2009 it was completely rebuilt by Victorian locomotive restoration experts at chartered surveyor and globetrotting steam aficionado Bill Parker's Flour Mill Colliery workshops at Bream in the Forest of Dean, not only with a new boiler, but also new frames, the component which gives a locomotive its identity before returning to steam the following February.

Richard Trevithick's first public demonstration of a steam locomotive on 21 February 1804 is generally held to be the start of the steam railway era. His locomotive helped ironworks-owner

The replicas of the Steam Elephant *and* Locomotion No. 1 *on the Pockerley Waggonway.* BEAMISH

Samuel Homfray win a 500-guinea bet that a steam engine could haul ten tons of iron over the 9-mile horse tramroad linking Penydarren ironworks to the Glamorganshire Canal at Abercynon. Around 70 people unofficially hitched a ride on the train.

A replica built in 1981 by staff at the former Welsh Industrial and Maritime Museum, Cardiff, using Trevithick's original documents and plans is now on display in the National Waterfront Museum in Swansea.

The replica has been abroad twice to celebrate the 150th anniversaries of both the Dutch and German state railway systems. It also played a starring role in Railfest 2004, the National Railway Museum's celebration to mark the bicentenary of the original run.

A non-working replica of Trevithick's Coalbrookdale locomotive of 1902 was constructed in Birmingham in 1987 by Task Undertakings Ltd, partially financed supported by the Manpower Services Commission and the Prince's Trust, and is now displayed at Telford Central station.

Beamish Museum's working replica of Puffing Billy. ROBIN JONES

Two years later, a fully-working replica was built by apprentices at GKN Sankey in Telford in 1989, and is now at the Ironbridge Gorge Museum.

In 1992, a full-size working replica of Robert Stephenson & Company's *Planet*, built in 1830 for the Liverpool & Manchester Railway, was built by the Friends of the Museum of Science and Industry in Manchester.

Amongst the landmark innovations of the original was that it was the first locomotive to employ inside cylinders. Other improvements include a steam dome to prevent water reaching the cylinders, and buffers and couplings in a position setting a new standard.

Further 2-2-0s in its wake became known as Planets. The replica is now operated by volunteers at the museum, which includes the Liverpool & Manchester's original eastern terminus, and occasionally visits heritage lines for special events.

In 2002, one of the most remarkable and distinctive of all new-build early locomotives was unveiled by Beamish Museum.

The gigantic *Steam Elephant* – as opposed to an iron horse – was the early locomotive that the world had forgotten.

All that survives to tell of the existence of the original very oversize and unwieldy beast of 1815, very much a local and unique design by John Buddle and William Chapman for Tyneside's Wallsend Colliery, was a contemporary painting and a handful of basic sketches and other illustrations.

Indeed, the existence of the locomotive came to light only when a rediscovered watercolour sketch was exhibited in 1965. Its display prompted an elderly lady who had a detailed oil painting to give

The Beamish experts who built a replica Steam Elephant *had little more than this oil painting to go on.* BEAMISH

The replica of Locomotion No. 1 *on the Pockerley Waggonway at Beamish.* BEAMISH

it to a local school from which it was acquired by Beamish in 1995.

A remark made by the writer Stephen Oliver in 1834 also resurfaced. He said: "The great coalfield of Newcastle appears likely to be exhausted within 200 years. Shares in railway companies will then be at an awful discount and steam elephants will inevitably perish for want of food!"

From such scant evidence, combined with exhaustive technical research, Beamish experts produced a new set of engineering drawings and set to work on replicating this mammoth.

Much of the building was undertaken in the north of England, with the final construction and boiler testing taking place at modern-day locomotive builder Alan Keef Ltd's workshops in Ross-on-Wye.

The *Steam Elephant* now also runs on the Pockerley Waggonway. That is mostly where it will stay, for although many railways would love to take it on loan for special events, its enormous stovepipe chimney would not allow it to pass under bridges although a special visit to the Middleton Railway at Leeds was arranged for 2012.

Also in 2002, the Rainhill Trials of 1829 were 'replayed' at the Llangollen Railway for the BBC TV programme *Timewatch – Rocket and its Rivals*, using the replicas. The replica *Novelty* was brought over from Sweden for the event which, just like the original, was won by *Rocket*.

In 2006, Beamish unveiled a working locomotive of an early locomotive which had survived, but like the original *Locomotion No. 1*, is designed to remain a static museum piece.

The 2008 replica of Trevithick's Catch-Me-Who-Can, *with its wooden cladding fitted.* TREVITHICK 200

A fire inside the boiler of the new Catch-Me-Who-Can. ROBIN JONES

Prince Charles inspects the Planet *replica at the Museum of Science & Industry in Manchester in January 2010.* ROBIN JONES

Opposite: *The replicas of, left to right,* Rocket, Sans Pareil *and* Novelty *during the BBC* Timewatch Rainhill Trials *'rematch' at Llangollen in 2002.* PAUL APPLETON

The Shildon-based working replica of Sans Pareil. ANTHONY COULLS

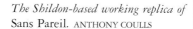

During 1813-14, engineer William Hedley, blacksmith Timothy Hackworth and enginewright Jonathan Forster and built *Puffing Billy* for Wylam Colliery near Newcastle-upon-Tyne. Used until 1862, when its design had long since passed its sell-by date, thankfully it was preserved. The world's oldest surviving steam locomotive, it is now in London's Science Museum, while its sister, *Wylam Dilly*, is safe in the Royal Museum in Edinburgh. *Puffing Billy's* place in history is hugely important, for the success of its design encouraged more local mine owners to look seriously at steam haulage, at a time when the British army was taking ever more horses and feed for use in the Napoleonic Wars.

The superb replica now rubs shoulders with those of *Locomotion No. 1* and the *Steam Elephant*.

Trevithick's last locomotive, *Catch-Me-Who-Can*, briefly ran on a circle of track in 1808 near the site of the future Euston station, and with its carriage, formed the world's first steam passenger train, and also the first to collect fares from passengers. It was built at Hazeldine Foundry in Bridgnorth, Shropshire, by pioneer steam locomotive engineer John Urpeth Rastrick.

For the bargain price of £50,000, a tiny fraction of the cost of building *Tornado*, a group of Bridgnorth residents formed a charity with the aims of building a working replica locomotive and organising events including lectures, concerts and outdoor events celebrate the 2008 bicentenary of this historic event, The Trevithick 200 group also built its replica in Bridgnorth and displayed it, part completed but with a fire in its boiler, at a gala weekend at Barrow Hill roundhouse near Chesterfield in September 2008. It has since had wooden cladding applied like the original.

CHAPTER FOUR
THE BROADER PICTURE

AS CHIEF MECHANICAL ENGINEER of the London, Midland & Scottish Railway, William Stanier designed some of the finest locomotives in the world, including the company's great Pacifics. He also wantonly destroyed two of the best. Long before Henry Ford, he believed that "history is bunk" – and consigned museum pieces to the scrapyard.

Do you recall the great video battle between VHS and Betamax in the 1980s? Betamax was considered the better quality by those 'in the know', but the big and bulkier VHS won the day because of a superior marketing strategy. The loser nosedived into obscurity and oblivion.

When Isambard Kingdom Brunel set out to build his Great Western Railway from Paddington to Bristol, he believed he could do better than George Stephenson's 4ft 8½in gauge. Brunel's system was built to 7ft 0¼in broad gauge – allowing bigger locomotives to carry heavier loads at higher speeds, and in many ways, it was superior to what came to be known as standard gauge. Brunel's GWR Locomotive Superintendent Daniel Gooch produced designs of locomotive which in their day were the fastest in the world.

The GWR and associated companies' broad gauge eventually stretched to Penzance and west Wales, and northwards as far at Wolverhampton. However, the big problem was the break of gauge: where broad met standard, passengers and goods had to be inconveniently taken off one train and on to the other.

The replica of Iron Duke *in steam at the National Railway Museum.* NRM

Iron Duke *inside the Great Hall of the National Railway Museum.*
ROBIN JONES

As the national rail network took shape, a Gauge Commission was set up to decide which was the best, and held a series of trials in 1845. The Parliamentary committee conceded that broad gauge had superior performance, but ruled in favour of narrow gauge, which was more widespread, and ordered no more broad gauge lines to be built – a ruling ignored by Brunel.

However, broad-gauge lines in Britain were gradually converted to dual gauge or standard gauge from 1864, and finally the last of Brunel's broad gauge was converted over a single weekend in May 1892. Virtually all broad gauge engines, carriages and wagons were scrapped soon afterwards, but set aside for posterity were pioneer *North Star*, preserved after withdrawal in 1871, and celebrity Iron Duke class 4-2-2 *Lord of the Isles*, the GWR exhibit at the Great Exhibition of 1851 in the Crystal Palace, and which was exhibited in Chicago in 1893 and Earls Court in 1897.

With space at Swindon Works at a premium, and no museum willing to offer either of the pair a home, when Chief Mechanical Engineer George Jackson Churchward was away on holiday leaving Stanier in charge, the latter decided to scrap both.

On his return, Churchward was horrified, and salvaged many of the parts of *North Star*, but could only save the driving wheels from *Lord of the Isles*. Stanier had no regrets, and when he took over the LMS, scrapped four historic locomotives which had also been saved.

The GWR was invited to take part in the 1925 Stockton & Darlington Railway centenary

Fire Fly rests outside the Burlescombe transhipment shed at Didcot in September 2005. FRANK DUMBLETON/ GWS

celebrations, but had no locomotive from its formative years.

The salvaged parts of *North Star* were tracked down and used in the building of a non-working replica at Swindon. It is this locomotive that is today exhibited inside STEAM – Museum of the Great Western Railway at Swindon.

The eighties, however, saw a broad gauge revival, in the form of new build. Retired Royal Navy Commander John Mosse was working as consultant architect to British Rail on the restoration of Temple Meads Old Station in 1981, when he dreamed up the idea of building of a new Firefly, a replica of the first one, but nonetheless the 63rd member of the groundbreaking class of 2-2-2 express passenger locomotives.

He soon found that many others shared his enthusiasm, including Leslie Lloyd, then general manager of the Western Region, his chief mechanical and electrical engineer John Butt, and retired railway engineers SAS Smith, who as manager of Swindon Works had overseen the construction of *Evening Star* in 1960.

The big breakthrough came when Daniel Gooch's original drawings for the Firefly class were found at Paddington. By 1982 the Firefly Trust was established and fundraising began.

It became clear that much of Gooch's specification would have to be modified to meet the needs of the safety-conscious modern world. These alterations included the braking, which on the original was not on the engine but on one side of the tender only, and the boiler, which Gooch had designed to be the main longitudinal strength member while additionally taking all the horizontal drag loads. Nor was there provision for boiler expansion.

The frame was redesigned to act as a support to the boiler rather than the other way round, with boiler expansion being permitted by the introduction of a dummy firebox, which would also take the drag loading. The frame, although considerably stronger than that of Gooch's, would still be true to the appearance of the original.

By 1987, sufficient money had been raised to allow building to start, as a Manpower Services Community project backed by Bristol City Council, but within a year, the council funding was lost and the group were forced to leave its riverside workshop when it was declared unsafe.

Help was at hand in the form of the Great Western Society, a group dedicated to the preservation of everything from the company whose name itself may have been suggested by Isambard. The society offered space in its new locomotive workshop at Didcot Railway Centre.

Meanwhile, the National Railway Museum commissioned a working replica of Gooch's first Iron

Duke 2-2-2 in time for the Great Western 150 celebrations in 1985, together with a matching open carriage.

It was built using parts from two standard gauge Austerity 0-6-0 saddle tanks, of which, as we saw earlier, a total of 484 were built, and with nearly 100 examples of them preserved, the loss of two was considered to be no detriment to railway heritage.

The new *Iron Duke* was built using modern materials and methods to exactly resemble Gooch's 1847 drawings, complete with exposed wooden lagging.

A short demonstration running line was built at the York museum to allow it to run, while Didcot

Fire Fly *hauls a replica broad gauge train over the Didcot demonstration line in April 2010.* FRANK DUMBLETON/GWS

also built its own broad gauge track, complete with mixed gauge section and the transhipment shed from Burlescombe, where in the days of the break of gauge, passengers and goods were switched from one train to another.

Following the untimely death of Commander Mosse, retired airline pilot Sam Bee took over as chairman of the Firefly Trust in November 1998,

Following the delivery of a new boiler from Israel Newton & Sons of Bradford and successfully steamed, the replica *Fire Fly*, built for a cost of around £200,000 over 23 years, not the 13 weeks and £1735 of the original, ran under its own power for the first time at Didcot on 2 March 2005. It was the first new main line steam locomotive to be built in Britain since *Evening Star* 45 years before, and the first express passenger locomotive since *Duke of Gloucester* in 1954.

Fire Fly's public debut came at the railway centre on 30 April 2005, when launched into traffic by 72-year-old veteran of film, TV and stage Anton Rogers.

Yet it will never be able to show just what the class was capable of doing, for apart from the two short demonstration lines, there are no other Brunel broad gauge railways in Britain. Nevertheless, thanks to the efforts of the new-build teams, what had once amounted to a quarter of Britain's railway network, a part which had in its day proudly led the world in locomotive technology, had been rescued from oblivion for future generations.

The 1925 replica of pioneer GWR engine North Star *assembled using parts from the original.* ROBIN JONES

CHAPTER FIVE
THE BEATIFICATION OF A HALL

DAI WOODHAM AND HIS LEGENDARY scrapyard at Barry provided many classic locomotives for preservation, which had they gone to any other breaker's yard, would have been cut up within days.

However, as we saw earlier, the fact that Woodham Bros was the only scrap dealer to have left steam engines to the last led to an imbalance in the types of engines saved.

Therefore today we have 11 GWR Hall class 4-6-0s, and seven of their successors, the Modified Halls, but no GWR Saint, Grange, Hawksworth County 4-6-0 or 4700 class 2-8-0.

Building a new one of each from scratch would cost a fortune. However, the Great Western Society realised early on that there was a quicker and very authentic way around the problem, drawing on Churchward's policy of using standardised parts.

The idea of recreating a Saint class was conceived by society member Peter Rich more than 30 years

After an absence of 54 years, a once-familiar classic GWR outline appears again. The partially-completed Saint No. 2999 Lady of Legend *stands at Didcot Railway Centre on 7 April 2007.* PETER CHATMAN

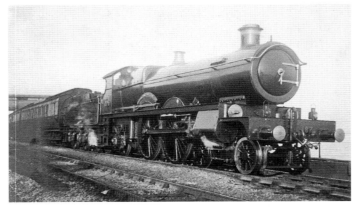

Top: *GWR 4-6-0 No. 4942 Maindy Hall on 3 June 2000, prior to dismantling.* PETER CHATMAN

Above: *Churchward Atlantic No. 187 Bride of Lammermoor pictured in 1909. The new Saint project is effectively creating two new locomotives in one.* GWS

ago, while he was rebuilding the group's Churchward 2-6-0 No. 5322 at Caerphilly.

While starting from nothing would back in the seventies be too big an ask for a locomotive of that size, he saw it would be an economic feasibility to turn a very similar engine into a Saint. He wrote an article in the society's magazine *Great Western Echo* to that effect.

The society subsequently bought GWR Hall No. 4942 *Maindy Hall* from Dai Woodham in 1974, with the long-term intention of turning it into a new Saint.

Maindy Hall had emerged from Swindon in July 1929 and was first allocated to Newton Abbot. Ironically, its last posting was at Didcot, where it spent its last year in British Railways service from November 1962. Withdrawn in December 1963, it arrived at Barry six moths later, and when bought, became the 51st locomotive to leave the scrapyard for preservation purposes.

The Saint or 29XX class of locomotives had been introduced in Edwardian times by Churchward. The Saint is considered to be a particularly important type in terms of locomotive development as it displayed many excellent features in its design which profoundly influenced the design of all subsequent successful locomotives built for British railways until the end of steam operations in the 1960s. A total of 76 were built.

The class was withdrawn between 1931 and 1953. However, by the early 1920s a great potential existed for a large mixed traffic locomotive which could work any type of train from an express passenger to a slow goods. Churchward's successor, Charles Benjamin Collett, decided in 1924 to rebuild a Saint, No. 2925 *Saint Martin* with smaller 6'0" diameter driving wheels and a more enclosed cab. This rebuild formed the prototype of the hugely-successful Hall class locomotives, of which a further 329 were built between 1928-50.

The initial detailed proposal by the Great Western Society which was made in the 1980s was to back-convert No. 4942 into a curved-frame Saint as it was considered that this would be easier. At that time there was considerable scepticism about whether the GWS had the ability and/or capability to undertake such a rebuild as nothing like it had been attempted before, and as a result the project failed to attract sufficient support.

However, when the idea was rolled out again in 1995 the decision had been take to rebuild No. 4942 as one of the earlier straight-frame Saints, and this time it received widespread support. The new plan also opened the possibility of running the new locomotive from time to time as a

Churchward 4-4-2, another extinct type, which would have been impossible with a curved-frame Saint.

The name *Lady of Legend* was chosen after a competition to name the new Saint had been held and was considered especially appropriate as the original 'Lady' series were the first of the straight-framers.

The number 2999 was the next available number in the straight-frame series, coming after No. 2998 *Ernest Cunard*. Some people argued that the new locomotive should be numbered 2956 as this was the lowest Saint number never to have been used, but this would have put it in the curved-frame series. As No. 2999 is essentially a new loco it is likely that it will carry a variety of different names once in service, and possibly the name *Atlantic* when running as a 4-4-2.

So the Great Western Society, which set out to save history and keep it alive, had embarked on a new path – to reverse it! A Hall would be lost, but its predecessor, a Saint, would appear in its place.

The aim is to recreate a Saint as it would have appeared around 1913, when the last Saint was built. Based on one of the first batches of Saints, *Lady of Legend* will feature straight footplating, correct type cylinders with inside steam pipes and lever reverse.

Much behind-the-scenes planning and design work was carried out by Saint Project engineering

Above: *One of the new driving wheels cast for the Saint project.* ADRIAN KNOWLES

Left: *GWR Saint 4-6-0 No. 2902* Lady of the Lake *heads through Acton with a Birmingham express as depicted on an Edwardian hand-coloured postcard. Note that the GWR carriages are painted in Indian lake livery, which preceded the more familiar chocolate and cream.* GWS

Below: *The overhauled* Maindy Hall *boiler for No. 2999 being restayed in July 2010.* PETER CHATMAN

manager Peter Chatman and other society members and a fresh appeal went 'live' in 1995.

The response was sensational. Money donated or pledged enabled an immediate start on the cornerstone of the whole project – the casting and machining of a new set of Churchward pattern 6ft 8½in driving wheels. These were completed in 1998 and both halves of the new cylinder block followed in 1999.

At the beginning of the new millennium the time had come to say a final goodbye to *Maindy Hall* which was dismantled and the original cylinders and frame extensions were split from the main frame.

Further appeals in 2002 raised enough money to ship the Hall's main frame to Ian Riley's engineering works at Bury where modifications to the Saint pattern were carried out in 2002-3. The main part of this work entailed removing 4¼in from the top edge of the main frame to accommodate the larger driving wheels and substantial repairs to cracking that had occurred way back in BR service, as well as manufacturing and fitting a completely new dragbox to replace the original

Saint No. 2904 Lady Godiva *heads through Kensal Green at speed.* GWS

The extension frames to convert a Hall chassis into one for a Saint. PETER CHATMAN.

Great Western Society chairman Richard Croucher looks out of the cab window of the new Saint. ADRIAN KNOWLES

that was badly wasted.

Extension frames were forged and machined and awaited fitting to the main frames at Bury.

The refurbished *Maindy Hall* bogie with new 3ft 2in wheelsets was then united with the Saint. For the journey back to Didcot Railway Centre, the boiler was mounted in the rebuilt frames, the net result being a rolling chassis.

In 2010, GWR 175 year, work was progressing on the boiler as well as the restoration of the 3500 gallon tender.

The aim was to have the completed Saint publicly launched at Didcot during 2013 – the centenary of the last Saint entering traffic, prior to main line certification.

A further dream of society members is to assemble a complete rake of Edwardian coaches to run behind the Saint, and several candidates for restoration and inclusion have been identified, although it would be highly unlikely that such a train would be permitted to run on today's main line.

CHAPTER SIX
GWR MIX AND MATCH: A NEW GRANGE

The cab of Betton Grange *on the frames in the Llangollen workshops.*
NEIL TILEY

WITH THE CLOSURE OF Dai Woodham's scrapyard on the horizon in the late eighties, there were still several rusting locomotives yet to find a home.

When the supply of Barry scrapyard engines dwindled to less than 30 by the middle of the decade, the former South Glamorgan County Council and the Welsh Industrial and Maritime Museum became sufficiently concerned that none had been earmarked for homes in Wales.

Ten locomotives, not the best of the Barry wrecks by any means, were bought by the council for £85,000 with grant aid from the former National Heritage Memorial Fund for a Wales Railway Centre proposed for Cardiff.

They comprised GWR 2-8-0 No. 2861; GWR 2-6-2Ts Nos. 4115 and 5539; GWR 2-8-0T No. 5227, GWR 0-6-2T No. 6686; WR Modified Hall No. 7927 *Willington Hall*; LMS 'Black Five' 4-6-0 No. 44901, LMS Stanier 8F 2-8-0 No. 48518; BR Standard 2-6-4T No. 80150 and BR Standard 9F 2-10-0 No. 92245.

In 1979, the Butetown Historic Railway Society had been formed at Bute Road station in Cardiff's docklands. The aim was to restore the then derelict Taff Vale Railway station, and establish a steam hauled passenger service to Cardiff's Queen Street station. By 1994, a short section of track existed, and the industrial Peckett 0-6-0ST No. 1859 of 1932 *Sir Gomer* hauled short passenger trains.

However, by 1997, the Cardiff Bay Development Corporation, by then given responsibility for the redevelopment of Butetown, and made it clear that neither the steam railway nor the museum longer figured in the plans for the area.

Although the local council retained ownership of the 'Barry Ten' locomotives as they came to be called, they were handed into the custody of the Butetown group after the museum plans collapsed.

With the Butetown society looking for a new home, in stepped the Vale of Glamorgan Council, which had inherited the ten locomotives. It offered the site on Barry Island to create a working railway heritage centre as a centrepiece in the plans for the future of the ailing resort. The society was repackaged as the Vale of Glamorgan Railway Company, later the Barry Island Railway.

The 'Barry Ten', which had been saved from the cutter's torch, ironically ended up back in Barry as a result, although for a few years they were stored in a warehouse on the Sully Trading Estate just outside the town.

The Vale of Glamorgan Railway developed a running line totalling around two miles in length, running parallel with Network Rail's Barry Island branch and linking Barry the town to the resort. However, funds were modest, and there was no hope of it raising sufficient money to restore even one of the derelict hulks, at a cost of between £300,000-£500,000.

For many years, the sale of the locomotives was out of the question, because the ownership became tangled up in red tape. The Heritage Lottery Fund, the successor to the National Heritage Memorial Fund, and the council would both have to give permission, and would need convincing that they would go to good use.

In the early twenty-first century, railway consultant John Buxton, whose firm Cambrian Transport now runs the Barry Island Railway, came up with the idea of not restoring all the ten locomotives in their own right, but again drawing on the GWR policy of standardised parts, to use components from each to recreate extinct types.

A shining star amidst the gloom of a dingy steam era locomotive shed is GWR 4-6-0 No. 6856 Stowe Grange. 6880

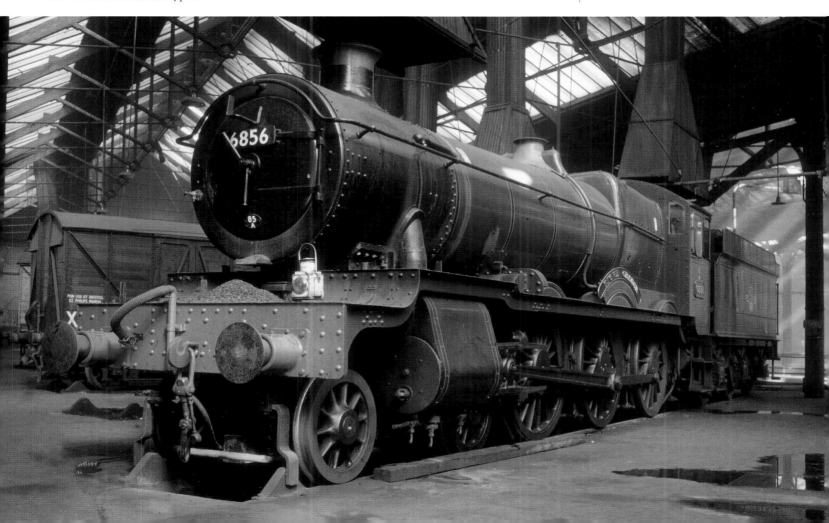

Above left: *Specialist welding being carried out on the Grange chassis.* 6880

Above right: *Project team members inspect the spare GWR mogul wheels at the Severn Valley Railway.* 6880

In what become known as the 'Three Counties Project,' John argued that sufficient components could be retrieved to build not only a Hawksworth County 4-6-0, but also the earlier Churchward County 4-4-0 and a largely forgotten design, the 4-4-2 County tank engine. Yes, the ten would be restored, but not all as themselves. Whereas *Maindy Hall* was being retro-converted to a Saint, some of the ten would be taken apart and reassembled in other forms, just like a pile of Lego bricks.

One glaring gap in GWR history was the absence of a Grange 4-6-0, which was broadly a smaller version of the Halls. Eighty were built between 1936-39, and they were reliable performers.

The author came across an Ian Allan locospotters book in which a large number of the Grange class had been underlined by his elder brother, during their lineside forays to Widney Manor station on the Birmingham Snow Hill-Leamington line in the early sixties. Sadly, within a few years all were withdrawn and cut up, Nos. 6847, 6848, 6849 and 6872 lasting until the end of Western Region steam in December 1965, but as with new build projects, there were those who were not prepared to let it rest at that.

The 6880 *Betton Grange* project started out just like most other 'new build' schemes; a group of likeminded people getting together with the aspiration of realising a dream to replicate some long lost class of locomotive. Only this one is different in many ways.

Firstly, the Betton Grange Society was formed by a group of people who had just completed the full restoration of a former Barry wreck, which was almost as close as you can get to being a new build. The rusting remains of GWR large prairie No. 5199 had passed 'around the houses' before a group of people, now the backbone of the scheme to build the 81st Grange got stuck in and turned it into a fully-operational locomotive.

No. 5199 spends most of its time between the Churnet Valley Railway, where it has been the mainstay of steam operated services in recent times, and its spiritual home at the Llangollen Railway, also home of the scheme to build Grange 4-6-0 No. 6880 *Betton Grange.*

The other thing that makes the *Betton Grange* project stand out from the rest is that thanks to the GWR's standardisation policy, the society has almost all of the components to build the locomotive, the main exception being the cylinders, which need to be cast from scratch.

Betton Grange was an early beneficiary of the Barry Ten when the society seized the opportunity to grab the boiler from *Willington Hall*, the main frames and remaining components going to Didcot to form the basis of the scheme to build a new Hawksworth County class 4-6-0.

One of the first priorities was to raise funds, and the society decided to recruit members willing to commit to £10 per month over a fixed period of time. To draw attention to the scheme, it was agreed to build the locomotive's cab first and take this around various shows to act as the backdrop to the society's fund raising stand.

The initial objective was to construct the main frames, so that it could be said that the locomotive existed, so once the cab was built, early fundraising went towards buying the steel and having this machined and drilled so that the locomotive's 'foundation' could be erected in the workshops at the Llangollen Railway.

It was also decided that the railway's engineering services arm, under the leadership of Dave Owen, would be contracted to build the locomotive to the exacting standards demanded of the Vehicle Acceptance Body and insurers, the plan being that when completed, No. 6880 *Betton Grange* will be a main line certified machine.

The main frame superstructure was completed in 2008 and soon the cab was fitted into place to give the impression that the locomotive was coming together at a good rate of knots.

Meanwhile the need for funds was pressing and although new express membership was now

The chimney from GWR 4-6-0 No. 6868 Penrhos Grange *has been made available to the* Betton Grange *project.*

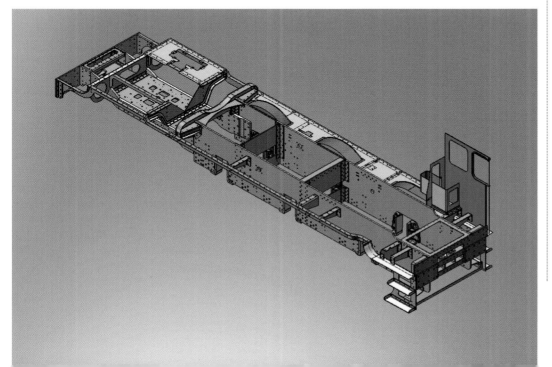

The GWR never had it like this: a computer-generated erecting plan for the Grange chassis. 6880

available at £68.80 per month, and the number of £10 per month memberships had grown significantly, a more substantial sum of money was needed to give a much-needed cash injection. And so the concept of the 'super gala' was born.

Unique among single locomotive societies, the Betton Grange Society ran its first gala at the Llangollen Railway in 2007. With an imaginative timetable and star-studded line up of locomotives, Steel, Steam & Stars as it was known was a resounding success and achieved its objective of raising a substantial sum of money to complete the main frames.

It was so successful that a second gala followed in 2009, only this time the format was extended to cover nine days and with the clear objective of raising £40,000 for the locomotive's extension frames. Again, a stellar line up of locomotives, including both the surviving operational GWR double framers, No. 3440 *City of Truro* from the National Railway Museum, and 'Dukedog' No. 9017 *Earl of Berkeley* from the Bluebell Railway, and LMS No. 6100 *Royal Scot*, went down a storm, with every B&B for a 20-mile radius full to sofa-beds.

Below: *The newly-cut frames for Betton Grange* displayed at the Steel, Steam & Stars gala in 2007. ROBIN JONES

Bottom: *A new coupling rod made for the Grange.* 6880

Sufficient money was raised to order the steel for the extension frames which were cut, machined, drilled and delivered by the start of April 2011. Plans were then made, Steel, Steam & Stars III to be held in April 2012 with the aim of raising up to £60,000 to get those cylinders cast and machined, with no less than *Tornado* and BR standard 4-6-2 No. 70000 *Britannia* topping the bill.

Meanwhile though, a major strategic decision was made by the Betton Grange Society's directors. Ken Ryder of the Cambrian Railway Trust decided he wanted to retire and offer his collection of locomotives and rolling stock for sale. The inventory included GWR 4-6-0 No. 5952 *Cogan Hall*, a locomotive type that had much in common with its Collett cousins, the Granges.

So No. 5952 was acquired, along with a large amount of spares that Ken had been quietly amassing ready for the day that the ex-Barry scrapyard locomotive went into the 'works' for a thorough restoration to operational condition. *Cogan Hall* moved to the back siding at Llangollen on 1 March 2010 and instantly there became a ready resource of parts to use in the construction of No. 6880.

However, it is important to point out at this stage that the society fully intends to restore *Cogan Hall* in its own right, once work on *Betton Grange* is completed. Parts will be borrowed, or copied as required to help speed along the construction. No. 6880 will then set about earning steaming fees to help its donor engine make its own return to steam.

Unrestored GWR 4-6-0 No. 5952 Cogan Hall *being taken from its long-term base at Llynclys near Oswestry to Llangollen on 11 April 2010.* 6880

With two boilers to choose from and a complete tender to go with the chassis already to hand, this project has really steamed ahead in a comparatively short space of time.

It has almost everything that it needs, and the speed with which funds can be raised is the only limiting factor.

Early in 2011, the bogie was removed from No. 5952 and moved to Williton on the West Somerset Railway, where locally-based society members stripped it down and started restoring it for use under No. 6880.

Back at the Llangollen Railway's workshops, the hornguides and ties, and the spring hangers, have been prepared to receive the 5ft 8in driving wheels which are due to be removed from the Severn Valley Railway following 30 years of storage. These were the original wheels from Collett 2-6-0 No. 7325/9303, which is on static display in the Engine House museum at Highley.

The locomotive received a replacement set that was in better condition from Barry scrapyard at the time of the locomotive's original restoration on the SVR. The old ones were retained 'just in case' but have never been touched since. Agreement was reached for the loan of these with custodians the GWR (SVR) Association.

With the driving wheels restored and the refurbished bogie returning to Llangollen, it was hoped to have a rolling chassis ready by spring 2012.

As the professionals at Llangollen carried out the heavier and more exacting work, the society's volunteers have kept themselves busy with the fitting of the steel footplating, priming and painting the frames and preparing the buffers for fitting to the extension frames, once they have been permanently secured to the front end.

Said to be excellent steamers and equally happy on fast passenger turns as they were on loose coupled or fitted freights, they were real favourites with GWR and Western Region footplatemen. *Betton Grange* is set to win new fans for the class, with a target date for its completion being set for 2016.

CHAPTER SEVEN

RECREATING HAWKSWORTH'S COUNTY: THE LAST GWR 4-6-0

The original GWR 4-6-0 No. 1014 County of Glamorgan *in ex-works condition.* GWS

CHARLES COLLETT RETIRED IN 1941, being replaced as GWR Chief Mechanical Engineer by Frederick Hawksworth.

At this time Swindon was busy building goods and mixed traffic locomotives to assist the war effort. Many of these locomotives were Halls, but Hawksworth decided to revamp the Hall design in the light of wartime experience and so, in March 1944, the first of the Lot 350 Modified Halls was outshopped. Ultimately, 71 Modified Halls were constructed, the last in November 1950.

Hawksworth's subsequent Lot 354 County 4-6-0 class was the last new design of GWR two-cylinder 4-6-0s and was therefore the ultimate development of Churchward's two-cylinder Saint 4-6-0 of 1902.

Introduced in summer 1945, they heralded a return to lined green locomotives on the GWR, following the end of the war in Europe. They were the product of a perceived need arising from deteriorating working and operating conditions during World War Two caused, largely, by poor coal supplies and a lack of skilled maintenance manpower.

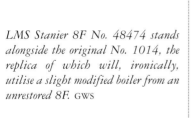

LMS Stanier 8F No. 48474 stands alongside the original No. 1014, the replica of which will, ironically, utilise a slight modified boiler from an unrestored 8F. GWS

While Hawksworth's first response had been the Modified Halls, with the end of the war approaching, and thoughts beginning to turn to peacetime operating conditions, a view developed that an enlarged boiler might be a further improvement, hence his new County 4-6-0s.

Initially allocated numbers in the 99XX series, the first of this new type appeared from Swindon in early summer 1945 as No. 1000, but without a name. Its appearance caused a considerable stir, as, despite the presence of many traditional Swindon features, there were also many new or novel ones, particularly the one-piece splashers, double chimney and flat-sided tender and later, a straight nameplate.

Many others were not so evident: driving wheelsets of 6ft 3in diameter, a new size for the GWR, the boiler pressure of 280 lbs/sq in from a new and larger boiler that must have challenged the GWR height gauge clearances, together with a wider 8ft 6in cab and corresponding tender.

A novelty was the fitting of No. 1000, the first of the class, with a double chimney, possibly based on that of the LMS rebuilt Royal Scot No. 1001, which followed, and all other subsequent 28 locomotives were built with a single chimney although all subsequently received a double chimney to a different design. From March 1946, they were given the County class name and all were eventually named after English and Welsh counties served by the GWR.

The dimensions of Lot 354 were very similar to those of the Modified Hall, but the main difference lay in the boiler. Classified as a Standard No 15 type OA, the new Lot 354 boiler was based on that constructed for a batch of 80 Stanier 8F 2-8-0 locomotives built at Swindon between May 1943 and July 1945 to fulfil wartime needs.

Although a thoroughbred LMS design, these locomotives worked on the GWR system following construction, not being delivered to the LMS until October 1947. While the firebox was of almost identical

The bogie of County of Glamorgan *being reassembled at Didcot on 30 July 2011.*
FRANK DUMBLETON/GWS

The new driving wheelsets for County of Glamorgan *at Buckfastleigh Works on the South Devon Railway.* GWS

The Stanier 8F boiler which will be used to build a new County, even though it is from a locomotive designed by rival company the LMS. GWS

dimensions, the Lot 354 barrel was longer than the Stanier boiler.

In addition to the substitution of the LMS boiler mountings by GWR versions, Hawksworth, influenced by Bulleid's work on the Southern Railway, also adopted a nickel steel alloy boiler pressed to 280 lbs/sq in. A three-row superheater was also fitted. The boiler and cylinders together provided a tractive effort of 32,580 lbs, greater than a Castle. The County's GWR power classification was E, later 6MT under the BR system.

Hawksworth's Counties were not universally liked. Footplatewise, the Counties were very similar to all their predecessors but, in service, it was evident that they were not fulfilling their potential, there being particular problems with steaming, subsequent servicing and rough riding which manifested itself in hammer blow on the track that did not endear the locomotives to the civil engineers. The latter was ameliorated by lowering the boiler pressure to 250 lb/sq in, which reduced the tractive effort to 29,050lbs and its GWR power classification to D.

In 1953, Hawksworth's replacement, Sam Ell, was allowed to tackle the draughting issues afflicting a number of former GWR locomotives, including the Counties.

Testing began with one of the poorest performers, class leader No. 1000 *County of Middlesex*, and an experimental double chimney was fitted to No. 1009 *County of Carmarthen* in 1954. Subsequently, revised double chimneys and a four-row superheater transformed the class and they became good performers.

No. 1014 was completed at Swindon on 18 February 1946 at a cost of £7,923 (£263,000 at 2011 cost), It was named *County of Glamorgan* on 15 March 1948 and fitted with a double chimney in November 1956.

It was withdrawn from service on 24 April 1964 having covered 756,762 miles and was subsequently sold as scrap to John Cashmore Ltd of Newport, South Wales, and cut up between December 1964 and January 1965. No members of the class survived.

Following the success of the project to reverse engineer an original Hall to a Saint, a Great Western Society member proposed that a similar exercise might be carried out with converting a Modified Hall to a County, further demonstrating the lineage and ultimate development of the 4-6-0 two-cylinder locomotive, and again, filling a sizeable gap in locomotive history.

Rather than number the new locomotive 1030 and to struggle to find another GWR connected county, it was decided to title it No. 1014 *County of Glamorgan*, to reflect the links with that Welsh county, its institutions and Dai Woodham's scrapyard.

As already mentioned, the Modified Halls and the Counties shared many similarities, with almost identical bogies and similar frames, cylinders and motion.

Modified Hall No. 7927 *Willington Hall* is a central plank of the scheme to build a new

Below left: *A new coupling rod for No. 1014 being forged.* GWS

Below right: *The completed new exhaust chest.* GWS

Hawksworth County, in mid-1950s Western Region condition, with a double chimney and a three-row superheater, to operate on the main line. After the Grange project took its boiler, the frames went to the County project, while Stanier 8F No. 48518 from the 'Barry Ten' has donated its very similar boiler.

The project has been divided into four phases: modification of the frames and manufacture of three new driving wheelsets, rebuilding the 8F boiler to a No. 15 OA boiler with double chimney, acquisition/refurbishment of the motion, manufacture of the fittings and pipework and construction of a new flat sided tender.

The frames of No. 7927 were converted to County specification at the Llangollen Railway workshops during 2005/6 following their repatriation from Barry, and the rebuild has been progressing at Didcot since 2007. New footplating and splashers have been fitted, together with new sandboxes and linkages, while work has started on the cab and reverser mechanism, which has included a new reverser pedestal.

The hornguides have been refurbished and the axleboxes await machining to take the new driving wheelsets. New main springs have also been manufactured while those for the tender and bogie have been refurbished.

It is hoped that No. 1014 will be rewheeled during 2012. Donor parts are still being acquired, conditioned and repaired or reconditioned; and other components are being designed and manufactured using the vast GWR drawing database that the project team have created.

Work has been progressing on construction of the new Hawksworth tender. The County tenders were 6in wider than those constructed for other classes such as the later Castles and the Modified Halls. The society has an unrestored Collett tender, which has been used as a parts donor for a new one for No. 1014.

One major design challenge is to redesign the frame mounts for the boiler and smokebox so that the gauging is compatible with the current Network Rail parameters. This involves a reduction of the boiler centreline by 1.75in and corresponding reductions at the cab shoulder and at the top of the tender side sheets to achieve a total height reduction of a whisker under 4in.

Regarding completion, at the time of writing, all the team would say is that 2015 will be a very significant year for the project.

The main frame of the tender being built for No. 1014 at Didcot. GWS

CHAPTER EIGHT
TORNADO THE MAGNIFICENT!

THERE IS LITTLE DOUBT that new £3-million A1 Pacific No. 60163 *Tornado* is now not only flying the flag for the new-build movement, but for the railway heritage sector as a whole. Not since the days of steam has a single new locomotive ignited such international interest amongst the public at large, from the Royal Family downwards.

As a new-build project, *Tornado* ticks all the boxes and more besides. Many a scheme has been mooted, but builder The A1 Steam Locomotive Trust is the first to pioneer the way to main line certification.

From the outset, there are many who said it couldn't be done. However, initial pure enthusiasm for the recreation of a much-loved post-war express passenger locomotive type translated itself not only into a sheaf of blueprints for tackling the job in stages, but most importantly of all, a groundbreaking fundraising programme.

In April 1990, enthusiast Mike Wilson of Stockton-on-Tees proposed in the now-defunct fortnightly newspaper *Steam Railway News* that a group should be set up to build a new Peppercorn Pacific.

Reading his words were the Champion brothers David and Phil. David has been considering the idea of new-build since the sixties.

He had seen Mike Satow's building of replica locomotives from the dawn of steam and the new Ffestiniog double Fairlie emerge in 1979. By that time, the restoration of No. 71000 *Duke of Gloucester* had proved it was possible to make so many new components that it was feasible to build an entire new locomotive.

The brothers wrote to Mike offering to join the project, and David recruited locomotive engineer Ian Storey and Newcastle-upon-Tyne lawyer Stuart Palmer. The five of them launched the project in York at the end of 1990, after the National Railway Museum confirmed that all the A1 drawings still existed.

David realised that it was not enough to build a replica A1 Pacific. It had to be the next A1 Pacific, the 50th member of the class, thereby allowing small changes to be made to the original design to meet modern standards. It would be numbered next in the class after No. 60162 *Saint Johnstoun*.

He also drew up the simple but hugely-effective plan whereby covenators would be recruited to

Smoke envelops A1 Trust chairman Mark Allatt inside Darlington Locomotive Works after the first fire was lit in Tornado's *firebox on 9 January 2008.* ROBIN JONES

A1 Peppercorn Pacific No. 60163 Tornado *passes Darnholm during a visit to the North Yorkshire Moors Railway on 31 May 2011.* ALAN WEAVER/A1SLT

Tornado *unveiled to the world's media at Darlington on 1 August 2008.*
ROBIN JONES

fund part of the cost. All they had to do was to give the price of a pint of beer a week.

Six days after the trust was launched, around 120 people packed out the inaugural meeting at the Railway Institute in York on 17 November 1990. So great was the attendance that people were standing on the stairs outside. David himself signed the first covenant, and within 30 minutes, 100 people had also signed up, while several top quality professional people came on board – Barry Wilson, then vice-president of Bank of America in Jersey, Wreford Voge, an accountant and expert on charities from Edinburgh, aero industry engineer David Elliott and marketing man Mike Fanning from Doncaster.

Two years later, marketing expert and future A1 Trust chairman Mark Allatt came on board, to be joined by experienced project planner Rob Morland and then Andrew Dow, the previous head of the National Railway Museum.

Four years later, the first and last components, a bogie swivel pin and a regulator nut, were unveiled. On 22 April, building began with the rolling of the frame plates at Scunthorpe.

In January 1995, the nameplates were presented at the frame laying ceremony, and also that year, the first wheel was cast.

In its early stages, the project progressed at Tyseley Locomotive Works under the watchful eye of chief engineer Bob Meanley. It was there that three cylinder castings unveiled on 25 May 1997.

Tornado *pulled its first passenger train on the Great Central Railway on 21 September 2009.* ROBIN JONES

Left: *Undertaking a test run after boiler repairs, Peppercorn A1 Pacific No. 60163* Tornado *stands at York on the evening of 18 May 2011.* JACK BEESTON/A1 SLT

Opposite: *British Railways A1 Pacific No. 60131 Osprey at Wakefield Westgate station. This photograph is part of the collection at the National Railway Museum, nowadays a primary base for* Tornado *and where it can often be seen on display when not working.* NRM

Above from left to right:
Among those on the first passenger train hauled by Tornado *was one of the project founders, David Champion, who brought along his dog Bud wearing a 60163 jacket!* ROBIN JONES

The A1 Steam Locomotive Trust president Mrs Dorothy Mather, widow of designer Arthur H. Peppercorn. ROBIN JONES

The A1 Steam Locomotive Trust's director of engineering David Elliott, the man who made so much of Tornado *happen mechanically, outside the door to Darlington Locomotive Works.* ROBIN JONES

In March 1997, the frame was displayed at the Great Hall at the National Railway Museum at York, and also that year, the project moved to the former Hopetown Carriage Works at Darlington North Road station. The carriage works then became Darlington Locomotive Works.

By 2000, half of the building was complete, and in 2004, it had become a rolling chassis. The biggest job of all was the boiler, and after failing to find a British manufacturer, and raising more finance through commercial loans, a contract was placed with Dampflokomotiv Meiningen, part of the former East German railway system which had continued with steam engineering.

In June 2007, the boiler and firebox assembly were fitted to the frames, and on 9 January 2008, the author had the honour of being invited to help push the locomotive out of the works into the sunshine after a fire had been lit in its boiler.

The tender was finished that February, and still in grey primer, *Tornado* was publicly unveiled to the media outside the works on 1 August, moving up and down on its short length of track.

It was afterwards taken to the Great Central Railway at Loughborough for running in. It was there on 21 September that it hauled its first passenger train.

All being well, it was moved to the NRM from where main line test runs began on 4 November, still in the grey undercoat. The third and final main line test run was completed on 19 November.

The fact that each of these stages was groundbreaking in its own right cannot be overstated. The

A1 Trust was not only turning its own dream into reality but blazing a trail often through red tape for others to follow.

It was on 13 December that it was unveiled in its first livery, British Railways apple green. And on 31 January 2009, excitement reached fever pitch along the East Coast Main Line from York to Newcastle-upon-Tyne, where spectators and cameramen grabbed every vantage point to glimpse its first passenger train, 'The Peppercorn Pioneer.' A week later, on 7 February, *Tornado* ran for the first time into that hallowed cathedral of steam, King's Cross, hauling the 'Talisman' from Darlington.

On 14 February, No. 60163 became the first of the 50 A1s to run on the Southern Region, when it made its first departures from the capital, from Waterloo and Victoria, 14 February.

The crowning glory came on 19 February when *Tornado* was officially named by Prince Charles and the Duchess of Cornwall, at York, before being given the rare honour of hauling the Royal Train, to Leeds, with the prince in a boiler suit on the footplate. Amongst the proudest people on the York platform that day was Mrs Dorothy Mather, the widow of designer Arthur H. Peppercorn who had passed away 56 years before. Dorothy, the trust's president, had also lit the first fire in it on 9 January 2008.

On 28 February, No. 60163 made it first journey into Scotland with 'The Auld Reekie Express' from York to Edinburgh, and on 7 March, it became the first A1 out of Edinburgh for 40 years with the 'North Briton' back to York. On 18 April, it became the first A1 to run out of King's Cross for 40 years.

Its celebrity status came to the fore on 25 April 2009, when it hauled a ten-coach private charter from King's Cross to Edinburgh amidst tight secrecy. The train was filmed for the BBC motoring show *Top Gear* and was taking part in a race. Presenter Jeremy Clarkson shovelled coal on the footplate as *Tornado* raced colleagues James May in a Jaguar XK120 along the A1 and Richard Hammond on a Vincent Black Shadow motorbike. Due to delays entering Edinburgh, *Tornado* came second and the motorbike third. The show was screened on 21 June 2009.

By then, the whole nation had become fascinated by the gleaming new locomotive. Such excitement recalled the days when big glamorous express locomotives featured on the cover of *Boy's Own*. Wherever it went, crowds packed stations to see it steam in and out.

On 8 August, it made its first visit to Plymouth, hauling 'The Tamar Tornado.' On 4 September, it hauled the British leg of the 'Winton Train' from Harwich to London Liverpool Street. This was a modern staged 'replay' of a mercy train organised by British stockbroker Sir Nicholas George Winton MBE, dubbed the 'British Schindler', taking 669 mostly Jewish children from Nazi-occupied Czechoslovakia on the eve of the World War Two to safety in Britain.

Its first venture over the spectacular Settle and Carlisle route came on 3/4 October and its first run over Shap summit on the West Coast Main Line followed a week later.

On 21 December, with the author and his actress daughter Vicky amongst the invited guests on board, *Tornado* hauled a Steam Dreams Christmas luncheon train from Waterloo around Kent to Dover and back. Severe winter weather meant that the modern-day diesel multiple units which form the backbone of commuter services could not run – but an A1 could! Stranded commuters were allowed to hop on board the steam special to get home.

Autograph hunters mobbed the footplate crew including operations director Graeme Bunker after the inaugural 'Peppercorn Pioneer' on 31 January 2009 returned to York.
ROBIN JONES

Watched by A1 Trust chairman Mark Allatt, Prince Charles performed the official naming of Tornado on 4 February 2009. The locomotive is named after the RAF Panavia Tornado jet. NEIL WHITAKER/A1SLT

Barrow Hill roundhouse's LNER II gala on 4-5 April 2009 saw a unique line-up of East Coast Main Line steam power in, left to right, LNER A4 No. 6009 Union of South Africa, *A2 No. 60532* Blue Peter, *A4 No. 6007* Sir Nigel Gresley *and* Tornado. ROBIN JONES

On 4 February 2010, *Tornado* again, by request, hauled the Royal Train with Prince Charles and the Duchess of Cornwall on board, this time to the Museum of Science & Industry in Manchester.

Two days later at York, the Heritage Railway Association presented The A1 Steam Locomotive Trust with its highest accolade, the Peter Manisty Award, in recognition of its unique accomplishment in raising the profile of the British railway heritage movement to the general public and throughout the world.

The achievements did not stop there. On 24 June 2010, *Tornado* beat the previous record for the fastest steam-hauled railtour over Shap summit by 19 seconds.

It was unveiled in lined Brunswick green, a popular choice amongst enthusiasts, at the NRM on 9 February 2011. The trust has said it will appear during its first ten years in all four liveries that the A1s appeared in their working lives.

However, early 2011 saw the locomotive out of action as the boiler was returned to Meiningen for repairs, but it returned and passed its steam test in April.

Modelmaker Bachmann had already produced one of its OO gauge A1 models as *Tornado*, but in summer 2011, Hornby honoured the project by turning out three different models, after measuring tornado itself. One, a limited edition of 1200, had *Tornado* in BR apple green livery, the second, coming as part of a train set with three BR maroon coaches, was saw it in Brunswick green. A third, aimed at youngsters as part of its budget-price Railroad range, was a less-detailed version in BR apple green.

At the same time, Bachmann announced an N gauge model of *Tornado* in BR green.

The headboard for the 'Winton Train' which recalled the Kindertransport of 1939. SP SMILER/CREATIVE COMMONS

So *Tornado* was all set to make its mark in the living room as well as on the main line.

Theoretically capable of 100mph, *Tornado* may gain permission to run at 90mph, making it the fastest steam locomotive on the British national network. There has also been talk about one day taking it to run on the continent where higher speeds may be permitted.

Tornado proved on a snowbound 21 December 2009 that it could do what modern trains could not in wintry weather – take evening commuters home. It is seen earlier the same day passing Staplehurst. A1SLT

During a railtour to Swanage, Tornado comes face to face with Another Pacific in the form of Bulleid Battle of Britain No. 34070 Manston. AMDREW P.M. WRIGHT

On 21 September 2010, Tornado hauled the longest public steam day excursion since 1968, all 505 miles from Crewe via Manchester, Shap and Beattock to Glasgow, and back via Wigan.

Whatever happens, thanks to the realisation of an 18-year dream, *Tornado* has proved that a new British steam locomotive, as in the heydays of the 1930s when the LNER and LMS Pacifics competed in the latest 'race to the north', can be an inspiration to everyone, whether they are railway enthusiasts or not. Especially with regard to the trust's fundraising mechanism, its success has mapped out a way forward for new-build projects which challenges others to better it.

CHAPTER NINE
A BR STANDARD 3 TANK – THE PERFECT CHOICE?

A SCHEME TO BUILD A NEW example of the extinct British Railways 3MT 2-6-2 tank engine, No, 82045 was first conceived by South Devon Railway fireman John Besley in 1988, during a conversation with the author.

Later taken under the stewardship of Severn Valley Railway enginemen Tony Massau and Chris Proudfoot, it took off at the end of 2008 when the finished frame plates for the new engine were delivered to the group's site at Bridgnorth. Since then, progress on this most practical of new-build locomotives has been rapid.

The Riddles Class 3 tanks – and their mogul sisters in the 77XXX class – somehow slipped through the preservation net in the 1960s, and all of them went to the scrapyard. Three of the tanks survived until as late as October 1968, but no white knight was forthcoming and they, too, were consigned to oblivion: a great pity, as these smart little engines would have been ideally suited to conditions on today's heritage-era lines.

The 82045 Locomotive Fund, as the group was initially called, was reconstituted as a company limited by guarantee in April 2009 and gained charitable status in January the following year, accompanied by a change of name to The 82045 Steam Locomotive Trust. Its stated aim is to build the

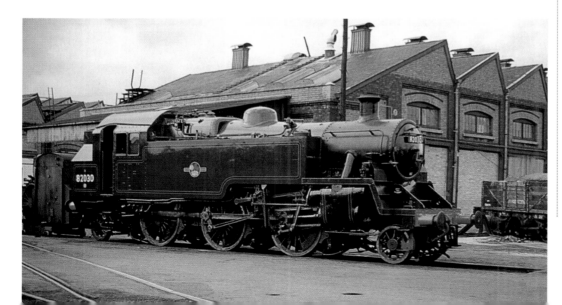

BR Standard 3MT 2-6-2T No. 82030 outside Swindon Works on 18 October 1959. RL COOK/82045 SLT

65

The chassis of No. 82045 awaiting the final stretchers including the smokebox saddle. 82045 SLT

next member of the extinct Riddles class (the BR engines finished at 82044) specifically for heritage line use and with no plans to run on the main line – unless, of course, a potential benefactor wishes to see this happen and is prepared to put up the necessary cash. When completed, it will run both on the SVR and visit other heritage lines.

Project engineer Tony Massau, who is also a professional engineer, had considered for many years that Standard 3 tanks would be an ideal engine for average-sized heritage lines, because of their economical size.

Around the original partnership has grown a multi-talented team of SVR volunteers, and the trust now boasts three skilled engineers (including an expert machinist), a Lloyds coded welder, a patternmaker and an enthusiastic weekly working party co-ordinator in Colin Williams, a Severn Valley veteran.

The trust has taken care to remain solvent, and is able to budget forward on the basis of assured monthly income. The estimated total cost of building No. 82045 is expected to be around £1,125,000, and the trust had by summer 2011 raised so far £150,000, a figure which can be virtually doubled when the large volunteer labour element is factored in.

At the time of writing, the engine's chassis is complete, all frame stretchers and horns in situ and the impressive smokebox saddle mounted between the frames. The riveting of the frame assembly is to be undertaken by the SVR as a contract job. The trust was about to place the order for making the pattern for the cylinders.

Hopefully the frames and cylinder assemblies will be complete by late summer 2012. Then, the trust will launch an appeal for the six driving wheels to be cast (the pattern is already available) machined, tyred and pressed on to axles; plus the front and rear pony truck assemblies completed.

A major problem facing heritage lines everywhere is keeping sufficient locomotives operational for services to be maintained; it is proving an ever-increasing headache as existing steam fleets rack up the years. Even the most-recently built BR Standards are now well past their half-century, while a typical LMS 'Black Five', for instance, is about 75 years old. The trust says it is not its intention that new-build locomotives should supplant their older sisters, but rather that they should help shoulder the burden of maintaining daily services and thereby prolong the working lives of the historic engines.

Once No. 82045 is well on the way to becoming a wheeled chassis, the trust will turn its attention to building the boiler and firebox. The decision has been taken to go with a traditional lapped and riveted boiler with inner copper firebox and firebox tubeplate, and the boiler may be built at the Severn Valley itself.

No. 82045 will emerge from Bridgnorth Works an identical locomotive (as far as this is still possible) to the one that should have been built by British Railways at Swindon early in 1956. The later members of the class as built had a slightly different boiler tube configuration and a larger-capacity coal bunker (the self-trimming slope at the base of the original bunker was done away with in order to allow for an extra three quarters of a ton of coal), and No. 82045 will reflect these minor changes.

The 82XXX tanks were an everyday sight on the Severn Valley line in BR days, so the engine will have the added attraction of being authentic for the heritage-era SVR, Trust member Paul Anderson was a fireman at Nine Elms (70A) from 1963-66 and regularly worked on them. He said: "They were lovely, perky little engines that did everything it said on the box. Disposal was a doddle, and you could finish a shift on one without feeling all wrung out!"

An estimate for completion of the Standard 3 tank has been given as 2016.

There has been speculation about batch building, if No. 82045 proves successful. Alternatively, much of the expertise might go to a future group interested in building an example of the now-extinct tender engine version, the 77XXX.

Membership secretary Barbara Massau said: "We have always known that our engine would never be the Belle of the Ball, and it has never been our intention that this should be so. What we are aiming to do is to build a practical, no-frills but nevertheless attractive modern steam locomotive which we hope will help take the age of standard gauge branch line steam forward for succeeding generations to enjoy."

Below left: *The newly-shotblasted smokebox saddle awaiting machining.*
82045 SLT

Below right: *Engineer Bryan Clarke checks the fit of one of No. 82045 left-hand side leading hornguides.*
82045 SLT

CHAPTER TEN
WHY A NORTH EASTERN G5 IS IDEAL TOO

WHILE THERE IS MUCH TO SUPPORT the logic behind the building of a new BR Standard 3MT tank, much of the same holds good for a far older design.

Advocates of the similarly-extinct North Eastern Railway Class O (LNER G5) 0-4-4T also claim that despite its much older pedigree, it is the 'perfect' heritage railway locomotive for the twenty-first century. Again, the argument runs that most preserved lines are of the branch line type, running short or medium length trains, intermittently double-headed to increase haulage capacity.

Dr Mike Wood and the Great Northern Steam Company staff on 1 July 2008. JOHN LEWINS

NER G5 0-4-4T No 468 with a train at the now-closed Croft Spa station on the East Coast Main Line south of Durham. PHOTOMATIC/ BEAMISH MUSEUM

Elegant, but simple in design and construction, a G5 has the capacity to handle four to five bogie coaches, unassisted, in an economic manner. The classic design proved extremely reliable over a lifetime of more than six decades.

Designed by Wilson Worsdell in 1893, 110 of these superb locomotives were constructed at the NER's North Road Works in Darlington between 1894 and 1901. They became the standard NER passenger tank locomotive until 1907. All but two of the locomotives survived into the 1950s, the last one being withdrawn in 1958. It is a remarkable fact that these locomotives ran for over 60 years, with very minor modifications, only to be withdrawn when replaced by the first generation diesel multiple units. None of these locomotives was preserved.

It was the dream of one man, Durham GP Dr Mike Wood, that this situation should be reversed and a new G5 locomotive born. He approached Mark and Keith Ashton at Great Northern Steam in Darlington to discuss its feasibility.

After many long hours of discussion and negotiation, Mike commissioned a brand new boiler design, to be registered at Lloyds. The boiler was to be a fully-welded design, built in compliance with all the current pressure vessel regulations.

Once the boiler design was accepted and fully registered, the Class G5 Locomotive Company Limited was formed, with Mike Wood as chairman. The company now has six 'major' investors who have each invested a minimum of £50,000 and an expanding number of ordinary shareholders, who have contributed a minimum of £5000.

Building the G5, main contractor Great Northern has been working in close association with David Elliott, *Tornado's* project engineer.

The locomotive will carry the number 1759, one of two G5s withdrawn and scrapped in 1948. It

Above left: The completed and painted bogie for the G5 on display at Locomotion – The National Railway Museum at Shildon. LOCOMOTION

Above right: A test fitting of the boiler and outer firebox on 11 March 2009. JOHN LEWINS

Below: The first bogie wheel casting on 4 November 2009. JOHN LEWINS

The cylinder block for the G5 being cast on 17 March 2009. JOHN LEWINS

The still-warm cylinder casting on 19 March 2009. JOHN LEWINS

is being built in distinct units, ie boiler, bogie, cylinders, wheelsets, frames etc. Each unit is to be paid for on completion. This system has minimised the risk to both the company' and its suppliers. The bogies, followed by the boiler, are set to be the first two units to be completed.

The main frames, along with buffers and buffer beams, cast iron cylinder blocks, safety valves, the Westinghouse pump, brake gear and tyres for the coupled wheels are in the possession of the company.

In February 2009, the company board took the major decision to build the locomotive to main line standards, allowing it to obtain certification to run on the national network.

However, this has significantly increased the final build cost, estimated in 2009 at £850,000. At the time of writing, more than half had been raised.

The company has more than 130 of the original set of drawings for the locomotive, while further extensive redesign and updating of existing drawings has been undertaken.

The incorporation of an all-welded steel boiler will not detract from the external appearance of the locomotive, which will appear as built in the 1890s, apart from the location of the 'Westinghouse' pump, on the front of the tank, rather than in the cab.

There will be steel buffer beams, rather than the original wooden ones. The locomotive will be fitted with robust group-standard buffers, rather than those originally fitted, which were of NER design.

In addition, the bogie design has been redrawn and updated to modern main line standards, as have the frames and wheelsets.

Reconditioned Ross-pop safety valves, a bell-type whistle, Davies & Metcalfe vacuum brake ejector valve, an air cylinder, as well as other vital components have been purchased, as have a Wakefield lubricator and a pair of Gresham & Crave lifting injectors, as originally fitted.

Both cylinder blocks are now fully machined, ready for assembly into the frames.

Patterns for the coupled wheels are complete and are at Boro Foundry in Lye, near Stourbridge, West Midlands awaiting casting, once funding is in place. The tyres for the wheels have been manufactured and are in safe storage.

The final locomotive erection will be undertaken at Rail Restorations North East at Hackworth Industrial Park in Shildon, in the old NER wagon works.

A Friends of the G5 supporters group has been established. It is estimated that the G5 can be completed within two years, once the final funding is in place.

The locomotive will initially be based in the North East, where the class once reigned supreme on branch lines, and will undergo trials on the Weardale Railway.

CHAPTER ELEVEN

THE SECOND *BEACHY HEAD*

REGULAR VISITORS TO HERITAGE LINES will readily identify the London, Brighton & South Coast Railway with a myriad of brightly-coloured 0-6-0 tank engines, like *Stepney* and *Fenchurch*. A total of ten were saved for preservation, along with an E1 and E4 tank.

However, outside the National Railway Museum, where Stroudley's first B1 0-4-2, No. 214 *Gladstone*, is prominently displayed, there are no other LBSCR tender locomotives. That is a glaring void in today's steam fleet, for the LBSCR made its mark not with steam shunters but fast expresses from London to the south coast resort.

It was Locomotive Superintendent Douglas Earle Marsh who produced the Class H2 Brighton Atlantics for express passenger work between June 1911 and January 1912. They were an immediate success and hauled prestige trains including the heavily-loaded Pullman services the 'Brighton Limited' and the 'Southern Belle', described by the LBSCR as "the most luxurious train in the

The original No. 32424 Beachy Head leaving Victoria Station on its last revenue-earning run, 13 April 1958. ALAN CHANDLER MBE

71

Looking down between the frames showing brake gear. DAVID JONES

Fitter Nick Davies with a pair of driving wheels for the new-build LBSCR Brighton Atlantic No. 32424 Beachy Head project, which are having the cranks fitted. ROBIN JONES

World". They were all named after geographical features of the south coast.

One Brighton Atlantic was withdrawn in 1949, but the rest continued in regular use until 1956. The last survivor was No. 424 *Beachy Head*, withdrawn by British Railways in April 1958, famous as the last of the type to run in the UK. Had it lasted two years longer, it may have come to the attention of the nascent Bluebell Railway, but it was not to be, and when *Beachy Head* was scrapped at Eastleigh in May 1958, the class was rendered extinct. Until now.

A project to build a replica of *Beachy Head* was launched at the Bluebell on 29 October 2000. It had its origins in the discovery and purchase in 1987 of one of the two Great Northern Railway Class C1 Atlantic boilers which had used for heating in a woodworking factory at Maldon in Essex, along with the acquisition of a tender underframe from a Class B4, and a set of tender wheels from a Class C2X, both original LBSCR locomotives.

The C2X tender had been based for some years at Guildford where it served as sludge carrier DS 70183 until being purchased by Dai Woodham around 1981. He felt that some of the locomotives in his scrapyard would have a better chance of being sold if tenders were available, but this one was sold on its own to Madame Tussauds for its Royalty & Empire Exhibition at Windsor Central station, where it was made to look Great Western behind full-size dummy GWR Achilles class 4-2-2 *The Queen* that had been built at Swindon Works around the same time. When this attraction closed, the tender was cut up and the replica locomotive was left on display at the station.

The first new parts to be made were the hornguides, spring hangers and supports for the tender as the initial plan was to finish that first before embarking on the engine itself. However two Bluebell volunteer pattern makers asked if they could help, so their efforts enabled the front bogie wheels to be cast followed by many further parts thus saving an enormous amount of money.

A partnership arrangement with the National Railway Museum resulted in many original LBSCR drawings being made available, which have been invaluable.

By 2002 it was apparent that a dedicated building in which to construct the locomotive was essential, so a site in the yard at the Bluebell's Sheffield Park headquarters was identified, and planning permission was obtained at the end of 2004. After frustrating delays with building regulations, a lightweight steel building was erected by March 2006 and officially opened by railway historian Richard Gibbon OBE on 11 June 2006 where the new steel driving wheels from Nortons Cast Products in Sheffield and the newly-delivered blank main frames, supplied by Corus, were on display.

Financial support came initially from the Bluebell Railway Trust which provided a start-up fund to launch the scheme and has also contributed 80 per cent of the cost of the building. Regular income is mainly from Bluebell

Railway Preservation Society members who contribute by standing order around £25,000 per year, or by individual donations. A successful sponsorship scheme raised over £150,000 and enables supporters to identify 'their' parts and receive an attractive certificate.

A major milestone took place on 1 October 2007 when the completed main frames were lifted upright and braced together - thereby officially creating the new No. 32424. Since then many parts have been cast, machined and fitted including cross members, hornguides and brake gear.

However, two major items have caused much consideration, these being the cylinder/valve chest arrangement and the motion rods. On the original design the cylinders and valve chests were two large complex castings which would have been very expensive to reproduce; and the forging of coupling and connecting rods can no longer easily be done in the UK. The solution was the use of the water-jet cutting technique both for the new design of fabricated cylinders/valve chest parts and the motion and associated linkages.

Design engineer Fred Bailey has been prolific in producing excellent CAD drawings from which machining could be carried out either in-house at Sheffield Park or by outside specialist machining companies.

Keith Sturt, previously works manager in the main Bluebell Railway workshop and now project engineer of the *Beachy Head* reconstruction, has been removing surplus parts from the boiler that were fitted when converted for heating use at Maldon, and has also been adding internal pipework that was different on the LBSCR version.

The bogie wheels and the trailing wheelset were assembled at Ian Riley's workshop in Bury from the castings and delivered at the beginning of 2011, while the main driving and coupled wheelsets had their crankpins fitted at the South Devon Railway's Buckfastleigh works.

It was anticipated that the bogie will be assembled quite soon and the frames lifted onto the wheels in 2012.

The locomotive will be finished in its Southern Railway/British Railways guise. A 'guesstimated' date for completion of the project is 2016.

CHAPTER TWELVE
BLOOMING MARVELLOUS

IN 1851, LONDON & NORTH WESTERN RAILWAY Southern Division locomotive superintendent James McConnell designed a series of powerful 2-2-2 express engines called 'Bloomers'.

The locomotives were considered ahead of their time, with high boiler pressure, hopper grates and experimental fireboxes. Their design was reflected in the evolution of other LNWR classes, although the last was withdrawn in 1888 and none were preserved.

Developed from a design of McConnell's predecessor Edward Bury, the 'Bloomers' took their nickname from women's liberation protagonist Amelia Bloomer, who wanted to reform contemporary female clothing so that underwear could be glimpsed. Amelia Jenks, an American, married a lawyer, Dexter C. Bloomer, and by the age of 33 in 1851 she had been editing and publishing a pioneering

Under-construction 'Bloomer' No. 670 inside the works at Tyseley. ROBIN JONES

Below: *New components for motion of No. 670 in the Tyseley workshops.* ROBIN JONES

fortnightly magazine for over two years. She shocked Victorian society by wanting to reform contemporary female clothing so that underwear could be glimpsed.

When a handful of young women appeared on the streets of London in loose knee-length frocks and lightweight pants down to the ankles, as she recommended, as opposed to tight-laced corsets with yards of flannel petticoats and crinolines, it caused a sensation.

At first many ridiculed the girls who were wearing Bloomers, but the fashion quickly caught on, in the year of the Great Exhibition. The word quickly passed into common usage. London theatres staged Bloomer farces, while a brewery clad all its barmaids in Bloomer costume. Anything novel and striking was likely to be labelled Bloomer, and when an example of McConnell's new 2-2-2 new engine – also highly unusual in appearance as it unashamedly showed all its wheels – arrived at Camden shed, it was obvious what nickname it would be given by the crews. It caught on so quickly that it was soon used in official correspondence, and the name firmly stuck.

The locomotives were considered ahead of their time, with high boiler pressure, hopper grates and experimental fireboxes. Their design was reflected in the evolution of other LNWR classes although the last was withdrawn in 1888. Despite their success, none was preserved.

A non-working replica 'Bloomer' numbered 1009 and named *The Wolvertonian* was commissioned

The 'Bloomer' built for static display in the centre of Milton Keynes.

by Milton Keynes Development Corporation for display at the new town's Station Square.

It was constructed in 1991 by engineering students with assistance from craftsmen in nearby Wolverton Works, the LNWR workshops which built 'Bloomers' first time round. Its official unveiling was performed by Jon Pertwee, the third Dr Who, who performed a classic bloomer by referring to "Wolverhampton's" illustrious railway history. The 'Bloomer' has since been returned to Wolverton for permanent display.

However, around the same time, Tyseley Locomotive Works at Birmingham Railway Museum hatched a scheme for a fully-working 'Bloomer' replica, No 670.

Two McConnell tender underframes completely authentic to pair with a 'Bloomer' were discovered at the closed British Rail motive power depot at Northwich and a third, which still had the brake gear complete with wooden blocks, was located at Machynlleth.

With the imminent approach of the 150th anniversary of the opening of the L&B in 1988, a £40,000 grant to begin work was obtained from Birmingham City Council.

The all-welded steel boiler was completed in 1987 for around £25,000, while the six steel wheels were cast by Goodwin Foundries of Stoke-on-Trent. The driving wheels were 7ft 4in diameter and weighed around 1.6 tons.

Cylinders were manufactured by Precision Machinery Ltd of Lye, West Midlands, while a neighbouring firm built the smokebox, and a new tender tank was constructed at Tyseley.

When one of the tender frames from Northwich was stripped down for renovation following acquisition of the pair, it was found to have the number 603 stamped on the steps, pairing it with 'Small Bloomer' No. 3, built at Wolverton in 1859 and scrapped in 1884 after being shedded for a time locally at Nuneaton.

However, subsequent lack of cash at a time when Tyseley was undertaking rebuilds of GWR locomotives for the main line halted serious progress on the project which has been taking shape at over the past 20 years as time and funds permit.

In 2008/9, donations and a legacy from Ffestiniog Railway architect Michael Seymour, totalling £20,000, were used to produce components for the motion of the locomotive, which by then was 90 per cent complete.

The project team has also been raising funds for the project by collecting old computer printer ink cartridges and recycling them.

When complete, the single will be numbered 670, the works' postal address in Warwick Road, Tyseley, following the LNWR practice of not having a numbering sequence for locomotives but often taking them from works numbers.

CHAPTER THIRTEEN
JOIN THE CLAN!

AFTER BRITISH RAILWAYS came into being on 1 January 1948, its chief engineer, Robert Riddles, was appointed to design a fleet of standard locomotives, coaches and wagons, which were economic to run, easy to maintain, with a high availability and shared interchangeable, standardised parts and fittings.

To cover all motive power needs, BR Standard locomotives eventually comprised of 12 classes and 99 locomotives, from small 2MT 2-6-0 and 2-6-2 tanks to the 9F heavy freight 2-10-0 – not all of them represented in preservation despite their comparatively late introduction.

Increased loads over secondary routes were frequently being double headed by regional Class 5 types, and a more powerful, more economic locomotive with a similar route availability was required. A large-boilered 4-6-0 was rejected as too heavy, so Riddles and his team decided to use a modified Class 7 chassis, fitted with a smaller boiler, creating a Class 6. The additional build and maintenance cost was offset against the savings on coal, and it was planned to build 117 in all.

The initial batch, numbered 72000-72009, were all allocated to the Scottish Region, and named after Scottish clans. The initial ten machines went straight into service from Crewe Works, missing out on their Rugby test plant evaluation.

The Scottish Regional Executive carried out road tests in service and their report was glowing, it revealed a fast, economical engine, light on both coal and water, able to run to, and make up time, "the steaming capacity of the boiler a revelation", exactly what an operating region wanted. The average coal consumption figures of the Clan, 31.8lbs coal/mile compares favourably even to the diminutive GWR two-cylinder 0-4-2T auto tank. Locomotive crews, especially at Carlisle Kingmoor, considered the Clans to be fine machines. They operated daily over some of BR's most testing routes, encompassing Beattock, Shap, Settle and Carlisle, and the tortuous 'Port Road' to Stranraer.

The main frames for Hengist. SSLC

Clan No. 72004 Clan Macdonald *at Shap Wells near Shap summit on 3 July 1954.* SSLC/NEVILLE STEAD COLLECTION

However, after the publication of the 1955 Modernisation Plan, all orders for new express passenger locomotives were cancelled.

As there were only ten Clans, the chances of an outstanding run by of one of these 'Cinderella' Pacifics being recorded by a student of locomotive performance was pretty low compared with its far more numerous big sisters, the Britannias, which were often hauling prestige named expresses. The official test runs were made under the scrutiny of a traction inspector who was not interested in spirited bursts of speed but consistent time keeping and economies of fuel and water and his very presence would have ensured the crew were on 'best behaviour'. However, an impressive run timed over the Settle and Carlisle was made by No. 72005 *Clan MacGregor*, standing in for failed Jubilee No. 45673 *Keppel* and 'Black Five' No. 45171 pairing on the 112coach 'Thames-Clyde' relief on the Settle and Carlisle line. A total of 141.5 minutes from Carlisle and over the Pennines to Leeds including temporary speed restrictions gave an average speed of 45 mph: today's quickest schedule, with modern diesel units is 149 minutes.

Sadly, no Clan made it into preservation. However, Paul Burns, a modern-day main line steam locomotive fireman and driver, who had worked the first BR Standard, No. 70000 *Britannia* on main line specials, found himself admiring the engine not only from an aesthetic point of view, but also from the design and work aspect, as a solution to a job to be done. The class's smaller sister, the Clan, became the focus of his attention. The National Railway Museum holds all the drawings and

Above, centre: The combination link is one of many components already produced for the new Clan. SSLC

Above, bottom: The patterns for Hengist's combi stretcher and brake cylinder support pattern. SSLC

The smokebox barrel at the South Devon Railway's Buckfastleigh works in 2009. ROBIN JONES

Artist's impression of the new Clan
Hengist. SSLC

also the revised drawings for the next batch of Clans, Nos. 72010-72014, *Hengist*, *Horsa*, *Wildfire*, *Firebrand* and *Canute*, which were never built.

In 1995, he and like-minded enthusiasts launched a project to build a new one, filling in a void left by what they saw as a very underrated and overlooked locomotive, under the banner of the Standard Steam Locomotive Company Limited. It would be numbered 72010 and named *Hengist* after what would have been the next in line at Crewe, adopting all the improvements outlined in the Lot 242.

Then began the hard work, developing a project plan, raising money, ordering drawings, and making parts. The adventure to build No. 72010 *Hengist* had started.

Great pains are being taken to produce a locomotive which is not a 'replica', but rather the true serial production machine in every possible respect, bolt for bolt, and rivet for rivet, just as British Railways had intended had political decisions not intervened.

Initially components were stored all over the country, until a small space at the Swanage Railway's Herston Works was offered. There, many parts were constructed, culminating in the front buffer beam, apron, valance and smoke deflectors being displayed at Barrow Hill in 2002.

The bogie frames, main frames and the frame extensions were all cut, machined and drilled. The smokebox barrel, door and ring were made. The cab structure was almost completed before the space at Herston had to be vacated.

In addition to these substantial items, all manner of fittings, and smaller detail components have been bought or made. All this was achieved through volunteer efforts through donations raised through the membership, the sale of railwayana, and *Hengist* merchandising, mainly casual clothing and the now familiar simple shed plate and numberplate fridge magnets. Since moving to temporary storage at Ian Riley's works at Bury, and the Shillingstone Station Project in Dorset, more items have continued to be manufactured.

The Standard Steam Locomotive Company has to be applauded for tackling a less fashionable locomotive, aiming to fill a historical gap rather than relying purely on popularity stakes, a big factor in the building of a Peppercorn A1.

CHAPTER FOURTEEN

TENDER LOCOMOTIVE
TO TANK ENGINE

AFTER A GROUP OF BLUEBELL RAILWAY members bought BR Standard 4MT 2-6-2T No. 80100 from Barry scrapyard, they went back to look for another locomotive. They were advised that BR Standard 2MT 2-6-0 No. 78059 had, as far as Barry hulks went, a relatively good boiler and firebox. However, it had lost its tender while had been converted into an ingot carrier at the steelworks at Briton Ferry.

The group nonetheless bought No 78059 which arrived at Sheffield Park on 23 May 1983. However, in the meantime, fresh discussions had taken place with regard to the engine's future. It

BR Standard 2-6-0 tank No. 84019 in Willesden shed. 84030 PROJECT GROUP

BR Standard 2MT 2-6-0 No. 78019 in service on the Great Central Railway. As three examples survive, it was decided to convert the fourth into the tank engine version.
ROBIN JONES

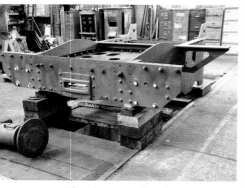

The almost-complete frame extension.
JOHN JESSON

was remarked that none of the 65 tender version of the 2MTs had ever worked in regular service on the Southern Railway, of which the Bluebell was once part, but members of the tank engine version, the 84000 class, had worked all over the Southern Region, having been firstly allocated to Ashford.

Also, there were three other 78000s in existence while none of the 84000s had survived. The decision was therefore taken to convert No. 78059 into the tank engine version, giving it the number 84030, thereby filling a gap in the preservation of BR Standards.

In all main dimensions the engines were identical, the difference of course being that the tank engine version had extended frames which carried the bunker over a trailing pony truck. In addition, of course, there were tanks carried on either side of the boiler/firebox.

At an early stage the group acquired a spare wheelset – believed to be from a BR Standard 9F 2-10-0 – as a basis for building the rear pony truck. All the wheel sets were sent to Swindon before the works closed in 1986 to enable the tyres to be turned and the journals attended to.

While various parts were being acquired the search was on for the relevant drawings to enable the frame extension and the trailing pony truck to be constructed. At this point a problem arose. While the workshop drawings for the frames were readily available those for the trailing pony truck were not.

It transpired that the pony truck was the same as that used under the Ivatt Class 2 tanks. Drawings for LMS locomotives are virtually unobtainable, so the group resorted to measuring up the pony trucks on one of the preserved Ivatt tanks and producing their own drawings.

Progress on the rebuild has been slow as the project team is only a small group who meet once a week. However the frame extension is virtually complete and the subsequent stage will be overhauling the axleboxes and hornguides so that the completed frames can be rewheeled, and producing a new pony truck frame casting which will shortly be ordered.

BR Standard 2MT 2-6-0 No. 78059 newly arrived from Barry, minus the tender. TONY SULLIVAN

CHAPTER FIFTEEN

"WE WANT OUR ENGINES BACK"

AN UNUSUAL MOTIVE for building two new steam locomotives lies in the hills of central Wales, and dates back to the dawn of the preservation era.

It is a case not of filling a historical void, but of a line wanting two of its original engines back – but cannot because they are now owned by its sister line a few miles away.

The operational railway preservation movement began when volunteers took over the Talyllyn Railway in 1951. They saved the line by the skin of its teeth, but were unable to do anything about

The first official service train hauled by new Kerr Stuart Tattoo No. 7 leaves Corris on 20 August 2005.
RICHARD GREENHOUGH/CRS

The original No. 4 with a goods train on the Dyfi Bridge in the late 1940s.
CRS

the nearby Corris Railway, which became one of the earliest British Railway closures in August 1948. At the same time, the two remaining Corris locomotives, Hughes 0-4-2 saddle tank No. 3 and Kerr Stuart Tattoo class 0-4-2 saddle tank No. 4, were in need of major overhauls.

The track was lifted by the end of 1949, but the two locomotives remained in their shed at Machynlleth, where stationmaster Campbell Thomas hoped they would find their way to the Talyllyn, which was also built to the very rare 2ft 3in gauge.

Indeed, in 1951, the newly-formed Talyllyn Railway Preservation Society bought the two locomotives for £50 the pair. At their new home, No 3 became *Sir Haydn* and No 4 became *Edward Thomas*, retaining their Corris numbers in the Talyllyn fleet.

In 1958, Talyllyn volunteers retrieved the remains of a Corris bogie carriage which had been used as a summerhouse in Gobowen, rebuilt it and returned it to service, allowing a genuine Corris train to be formed by adding the surviving brake van.

As the Talyllyn went from strength to strength, nobody considered that the Corris would be revived, as over the years, blockages had appeared on the route. However, in December 1966 a group of enthusiasts led by Alan Meaden founded the Corris Railway Society with the aim of preserving what was left of the line, opening a dedicated museum, and to perhaps reviving part of the route, maybe as a short demonstration horse-drawn tramway.

No. 7 hauls its replica Corris train through the spinney north of Maespoeth.
RICHARD GREENHOUGH/CRS

Selwyn Humphries, whose late father Humphrey drove the last Corris Railway train on 20 August 1948, in the cab of the new No. 7 at Corris station 57 years later. RICHARD GREENHOUGH/CRS

The society was subsequently able to obtain use of the railway stables adjacent to the demolished Corris station and laid a short length of track in 1971.

In 1981, the original locomotive shed at Maespoeth was acquired and became its operational base, and basic track was laid over the three quarters of a mile between there and Corris. 20 April 1985 saw Corris Railway No.5, a Simplex Motor Rail four-wheeled diesel named *Alan Meaden,* hauling a rake of wagons forming the official "first train" back to Corris, witnessed by former Corris Railway workers.

In autumn 1996, No. 4 made a brief loan visit 'back home' from the Talyllyn to celebrate its 75th anniversary.

Corris public passenger trains finally ran again, after a 72-year gap, at 11am on 1 June 2002. The following year, when the Corris Railway marked the 150th anniversary of its enabling Act of Parliament, the Talyllyn loaned its complete heritage Corris train, comprising No. 3 *Sir Haydn* (specially repainted into Corris Indian red livery), coach No. 17 and original Corris brake van No. 6.

Corris supporters then began to look at having an authentic stream engine of their own. They immediately realised that there was no chance of buying one of the two surviving original engines back from the Talyllyn, and so decided to build their own. They chose a replica Kerr Stuart Tattoo class locomotive as a substitute for the original No 4.

An appeal for funds to build the new engine, No. 7, was launched in 1994, and agreement was reached with former locomotive builder Winson Engineering of Daventry to construct the first all-new steam engine to be built for service in the UK on the rare 2ft 3ins gauge since No. 4 was delivered new in 1921.

One point that was decided early on was that the new Corris No. 7 would not be an exact replica

Corris No. 4 is now No. 4 Edward Thomas *on the Talyllyn Railway.*
ROBIN JONES

of No. 4, but a modern interpretation, so that improvements made to the prototype by the Talyllyn could be incorporated.

Fabrication of the sheet metal parts – cab, bunkers and saddle tank – was undertaken separately by society members and the completed parts delivered to Daventry. Finally, on 4 April 2005, No. 7 had its first official steaming in Daventry, and on 17 May, it arrived at its new home at Corris. The project had cost £120,000.

On 27 May, it hauled a train which carried the Welsh Assembly's First minister Rhodri Morgan over the railway. When No. 7 hauled a public passenger train for the first time, the 11am from Corris on 20 August that year, it was 57 years to the day since the final (freight) train ran on the original line. Among those present was Selwyn Humphries, whose late father Humphrey drove that last train in 1948.

Following the huge success of No. 7, the railway launched an appeal to build a second replica original locomotive, based on original Hughes Falcon class 0-4-2Ts No. 3, to take the pressure off No. 7. Again, modern improvements to the design of the original would be incorporated.

As no original drawings had survived, the original No. 3 on the Talyllyn had to be measured up to produce a new set, at a cost of £26,000. A decision was taken in 2009 to make the boiler the first item to be built and Israel Newton, a 200-year-old firm of boiler-makers in Bradford, agreed to build it for £31,250.00 plus VAT.

The first components for the new £250,000 engine were delivered to Maespoeth on 29 January 2011. They included the chimney and dome cover, and the boiler was nearing completion by mid-summer.

It is hoped to have the locomotive, which will be No. 10 in the Corris fleet, running in 2014.

Below left: *The chimney and dome castings for the new Falcon, No. 10.* CRS

Below right: *The completed boiler for No. 10.* PETER GUEST

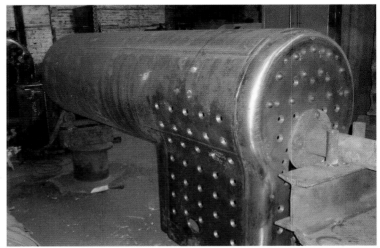

CHAPTER SIXTEEN
THE RETURN OF HUNSLET

ONE OF THE GREATEST NAMES in British locomotive building is Hunslet. Founded in 1864 at Jack Lane in the Leeds suburb of Hunslet by John Towlerton Leather, seven years later it was bought by works manager James Campbell.,

The first engine built in 1865 was *Linden*, a standard gauge 0-6-0 saddle tank delivered to engineering contractor Brassey & Ballard. Hunslet thereafter specialised for many years in shunting and short-haul locomotives, ideal for colliery railways.

Statfold and Jack Lane, *the first new Quarry Hunslets for three quarters of a century stand side by side at Statfold Barn,* HENRY NOON

In 1870, Hunslet constructed its first narrow gauge engine, *Dinorwic*, an 0-4-0 saddle tank built to 1ft 10¾in for the Dinorwic Slate Quarry at Llanberis in Snowdonia, Another 19 followed, and established the company's reputation as a builder of engines for use in quarries. The term Quarry Hunslet became used to describe several different types of 0-4-0STs, mainly used in the Snowdonia slate workings, and numerous examples of the 50 built between then and 1932 are represented at heritage venues today, both in Britain and in North America, to which several were exported after they were withdrawn in the 1960s.

The firm grew as a supplier of locomotives to many companies overseas, and also built engines for British main line companies, including 90 LMS 3F 'Jinty' 0-6-0Ts.

While several other British locomotive builders like Kerr Stuart and Avonside did not survive the depression of the thirties, Hunslet was quick to acquire their patterns, rights and designs. Also in the thirties, Hunslet carried out much work on the design of early diesel locomotives.

As we saw earlier, during World War Two, Hunslet designed the Austerity 0-6-0ST, building 149 Austerities during the conflict, while subcontracting construction of nearly 200 more. More Austerities were built and rebuilt after the war.

The first Hunslet engine built for export was 0-4-0ST No. 10, which was shipped to Java in May 1866. Ironically, its last steam locomotive, Trangkil No. 4, was supplied in 1971 to Java, bringing the curtain down on the British steam age, as far as building new locomotives for business, as opposed to heritage or tourist purposes, was concerned.

The Jack Lane works closed in 1995 after supplying a batch of narrow gauge diesel locomotives for tunnelling on London Underground's Jubilee Line Extension.

Today, the Hunslet Engine Company is part of the Burton-on-Trent based LH Group Services, Britain's biggest independent remanufacturer of power train products, which had been established in 1953 to supply repair and overhaul services to the 'off-highway' and agricultural industries.

Because of the acquisitions of the 1930 and later, it has the rights to locomotive manufacturers Andrew Barclay, Avonside, the North British Locomotive Company, Greenwood & Batley, Hudswell Clarke, John Fowler & Co, Kerr Stuart, Kitson & Co and Manning Wardle. Not only can it use these names, but can service and repair their products, and supply replacement parts. Indeed, Hunslet and its associated companies have produced over 19,000 steam, diesel and electric locomotives for destinations around the world.

Meanwhile, LH Group supremo Graham Lee built a sophisticated private railway at his farm near Tamworth, Staffordshire, where the main crop is seed oil.

Open to enthusiasts by invitation only on selected open days, the Statford Barn Railway has standard gauge, 2ft and 2ft 6in gauge running lines, as well as miniature train circuits.

Graham and his team have regularly scoured the world for redundant steam locomotives and repatriated them, rebuilding them at regular intervals to as-built condition in the Statford Barn workshops.

One such locomotive he brought back to Britain was none other than Trangkil No. 4.

Opposite: *New Quarry Hunslet* Statfold *in passenger service at Woody Bay station on the Lynton & Barnstaple Railway.* TONY NICHOLSON

Jack Lane *crosses the flat crossing when the Statfold standard gauge line bisects the dual 2ft/2ft 6in running line.* HENRY NOON

Opposite: Howard, *the first new Kerr Stuart Wren locomotive built by Hunslet, later renamed* Jennie *at the Amerton Railway.* HENRY NOON

Below: *Hardly the size of Crewe, Derby or Swindon, nonetheless the modest modern Statfold Barn workshop is, unlike those more illustrious names, turning out steam locomotives today.* ROBIN JONES

It had worked on a sugar plantation in Java for 33 years before it was made redundant, and was later acquired by Graham along with several others from the region. Originally built to 2ft 6in gauge, it was returned to England in 2004. At Statfold, during it overhaul it was regauged to 2ft before being returned to steam.

However, Graham did not stop at buying old steam locomotives, but went several stages further – and began building new ones. Not only that, but they were badged under the Hunslet name – and were the next in the production line from No. 3902, Trangkil No. 4.

The first emerged from the Statford Barn workshops in 2005. Named *Statfold*, it was nothing less than a fully-fledged Quarry Hunslet 0-4-0ST.

The reputation of the Quarry Hunslet for a combination of robustness, simplicity and performance made it the ideal choice for the twenty-first century Hunslet Steam Company's plans to resume manufacture of narrow gauge steam locomotives.

One would not be enough – and sufficient components for a batch of four were made.

Statfold entered service in 2006, and worked on the revived Lynton & Barnstaple Railway while visiting other destinations.

The next in line was named *Jack Lane*. There were key differences between the two, although they were constructed to the same basic design.

While Statfold has an enclosed cab, *Jack Lane* has an open footplate and a

taller chimney in order to keep smoke clear of the crew.

They were allocated works numbers 3903 and 3904 respectively, continuing the Hunslet steam locomotive numbering series.

Jack Lane was offered for sale in 2007 for £152,750, but at the time of writing there have been no takers. If you want a new Quarry Hunslet, the price quoted on the Hunslet website is £130,000. Of course, it is cheaper to restore an existing one, but if you are planning a theme park railway or private line and want an 'instant' steam locomotive, Hunslet is still a first port of call.

Next off the Statfold production line was a Kerr Stuart Wren 0-4-0ST, completed early in 2008 numbered 3905, and like the Quarry Hunslets, also a type already represented in preservation. The first steam locomotive built and sold by Hunslet in 37 years, it is now privately owned is based at the 2ft gauge Amerton Railway in Staffordshire, where it is named *Jennie* and forms part of the regular service trains. Another Wren, No. 3906, followed in 2009.

There is always something new at each open day at Statfold Barn, where more than 50 locomotives are now based, either in running order or in the restoration queue – and never forget, there are brand new parts to build even more!

Hunslet today offers a custom-design-and-build steam locomotive service to suit specific requirements, from 10¼in to standard gauge.

'ISSIN' SID – A LOAD OF HOT AIR

One of the most unusual locomotives to emerge from the Statfold workshops is *'Issin' Sid*, which has been built in partnership with owner Roy Etherington.

'Issin' Sid, is a replica of a 2ft gauge Lishman & Young compressed air 0-4-0 mine locomotive as used at the Earl of Durham's Lambton Collieries towards the end of the nineteenth century. The design was the world's first fireless underground locomotive.

Before flame-proofed diesel and battery electric locomotives were developed for mining applications compressed air provided a safe form of underground motive power that could be recharged from the same power supply as was used to drive drills and other machinery.

When the price of animal feed rose, mine owners began looking at sources of motive power other than pit ponies. By 1887, about 25 compressed locomotives were in use in the earl's collieries owned by the Earl of Durham, but their use in British coal mines ceased before 1900.

The very basic design was based around a wooden frame having dumb buffers which supported an air receiver with a capacity of about 25 cubic feet. Each locomotive had a pair of cylinders, each 3in diameter by 6in stroke, mounted between the frames and which drove coupled 12in diameter cast iron wheels with a wheelbase of 17in, to allow the locomotive to tackle curves of about 6/7ft radius. The forward and reverse motion was undertaken by slip eccentrics.

There were no springs on the suspension and the simple brakes were worked by hand at one end and by foot at the other end.

The total weight of the locomotive was less than a ton. They could haul up to four tons for up to 500 yards on one charge of compressed air, provided that the gradient did not exceed 1-in-48. They

Graham Lee, managing director of LH Group Services, who restarted Hunslet steam building 34 years on.
ROBIN JONES

'Issin' Sid *recreates a forgotten corner of British locomotive technology which had vanished from our shores by 1900.* ROBIN JONES

could be driven from either end but when hauling empty tubs the driver sat in the first tub to work the controls, but when hauling full tubs, he sat on a small detachable seat.

Compressed air for the locomotives was piped down from the surface at a pressure of 210lb/sq in. The filling apparatus was akin to a water crane, with the arm swung round to the locomotive to be filled and the valves opened.

Boys around 16 years old usually drove the smaller locomotives, and were able to undertake such work after a few hours instruction.

When six Lishman & Young compressed-air engines were exported to California in 1879, they became the first mines locomotives in the USA.

Roy decided to build one after he found a copy of Young's 1881 drawings and realised that the construction of an accurate working replica of the small type of locomotive was possible. Graham Lee offered the use of Statfold's workshop facilities at Statfold Barn, where staff including Stuart

Top: *A production line in progress: chimney caps for new Quarry Hunslets.* ROBIN JONES

Above: *A new boiler takes shape in the Statfold workshops.* ROBIN JONES

Visiting original Quarry Hunslet Jerry M*, now part of the Hollycombe Steam Collection in West Sussex, hauls a goods train on the Statfold Barn Railway in 2008.* MJ COGAN

Tomlinson and Richard Gooding helped him build the locomotive from recycled parts.

Roy wanted his locomotive to have a blacksmith's rough-and-ready look about it, not finished to the pristine standard of the Statfold Hunslets. Recycled parts were used: the frame was cut from the jib of a scrapped Smith steam crane and the cylinders, made by Holman of Camborne, were found by a dredger cleaning out the Kennet & Avon Canal in the 1970s!

The eccentrics came from an aborted project to install a steam engine in a canal boat.

However, new wheels had to be cast and Hunslet produced the casting.

Few mine locomotives ever had names, but as Roy pointed out, mining folk had a well-developed sense of humour and chalk was freely used underground, so the decision was taken to call it *'Issin' Sid* after the distinctive noise it makes, with the shorter form *Sid* applied in genuine NCB chalk!

The pit tub which usually accompanies Sid is came from New Lount Colliery in Leicestershire and is similar to those which came to be used in Durham. The locomotive has been allocated Hunslet works number 9902 in the Statfold special projects series.

CHAPTER SEVENTEEN
ANT AND *BEE*

THE ISLE OF MAN'S Great Laxey Mine was one of the richest and most successful lead and zinc mines in Britain. Its trademark is the great wheel, the 72ft 6 in diameter *Lady Isabella*, built in 1854 to pump out water. Mine shafts had been sunk to depths of over 2000ft deep and nearly 1000 men worked there,

In 1875, the year of its greatest output, more than 11,000 tons of zinc was extracted. That accounted for half of the total British zinc production.

The main level of the mine was known as the Adit Level and was 1½ miles long. It ran along the entire length of the Adit Level and was used to carry the extracted ore out of the mine to the "washing floors" where it was prepared for sale.

Ponies originally formed the motive power, but in 1877 they were replaced by two tiny 19in gauge steam locomotives constructed by steamboat builder Stephen Lewin & Company of Poole in Dorset. Named *Ant* and *Bee*, they stood just 4ft 9in tall, 3 ft wide and could pull up to seven of the mine's 200

The original Ant, *on its way back to the mine workings with empty ore wagons, as seen before World War One.* GLMR

New-build Lewin engine Bee, *with* Ant *behind, and three replica ore wagons.* Ant *and* Bee *had no cabs, and because of the low clearances in the mine tunnels, drivers had to remain seated.* GLMR

wagons each.

They were used until the mine closed in 1929 and were scrapped a few years later. In 1999, the Laxey and Lonan Heritage Trust began the restoration of the surface section of the old tramway, with the aim of having it running again by 2004 to mark the 150th anniversary of *Lady Isabella*, named after the island governor's wife.

The trust was not content to recreate a basic horse-drawn tramway, and so a fully-working replica of the original *Ant* was ordered from model steam builder Great Northern Steam Ltd of Darlington.

During construction of *Ant*, a decision was taken to build a replica of the second one, *Bee*. They were each built at a cost of just £30,000.

No original drawings for the pair survived, and because Lewin made only a handful of railway locomotives, precious little was known about them.

So a new set had to be compiled, from drawings for replacement boilers, safety valves and regulators supplied by WG Bagnall & Co Ltd in 1905, some dimensions given in a 1902 edition of *The Locomotive Magazine* and contemporary photographs.

The restored Great Laxey Mine Railway was officially opened on 25 September 2004, and the new *Ant* and *Bee* regularly haul passenger trains there. It is a classic example of a line's entire steam fleet being replicated!

CHAPTER EIGHTEEN
GWR STEAM RAILMOTOR: THE GREAT MISSING LINK

FOR ME, ARGUABLY THE MOST IMPORTANT new-build project today, in historical terms, has been the Great Western Society's project to rebuild an original steam railmotor.

What looks to the uninitiated as a wooden carriage which can move under its own power and makes the same sound as a steam locomotive will never for them have the immediate 'wow' factor of a gleaming new out-of-the-box express passenger locomotive like *Tornado*.

Yet it is the steam railmotor, not the big-name glamorous locomotives like *Flying Scotsman*, *Mallard* and *City of Truro* that explains how our modern railway system evolved.

Today, very few passenger trains on the UK national network are hauled by locomotives. Virtually all are comprised of diesel and electric multiple units, wherein the traction unit is contained within the train vehicles rather than being a separate stand-alone entity.

Self-propelled trains like multiple units can trace their ancestry directly back to the steam railmotor concept, which first appeared when engineer William Bridges Adams tested a handful of vehicles which had the locomotive physically joined to the carriage section in the late 1840s. The Bristol & Exeter Railway's broad gauge steam carriage was trialled on the Clevedon and Tiverton

GWR steam railmotor No. 93 on the Clevedon branch in Edwardian times.
GWS

99

branches, but the concept did not catch on. There were a few further experiments with all-in-one self-propelled vehicles in Victorian times, but the big breakthrough came when the GWR borrowed a London & South Western Railway railmotor for trials on its Golden Valley line at Stroud. It had the ability to stop at basic intermediate halts and generate additional local traffic far beyond the company's wildest dreams, and because there were cabs at either end, it eradicated the need for turning locomotives or them having to run round their trains before driving backwards.

The GWR liked it so much that it built two railmotors for the Golden Valley line which entered service on 12 October 1903 and eventually built a fleet of 99. The public loved the local and convenient services that they provided, and the railmotors were often packed to overflowing. Many of them also hauled trailers, making them the first multiple units, and seeing the success of the GWR, other railways all over Britain ordered their own.

However, they were the victims of their own success. They generated so much local traffic steam bogies inside them struggled to pull extra vehicles, and so a 'halfway house' compromise was reached with the GWR's development of the auto train, whereby a tank engine could be controlled from a cab in a carriage at the far end of the train.

Opposite: *Resplendent in GWR crimson lake livery, reborn steam railmotor No. 93 runs along the Llangollen Railway on 22 March 2011. It may have run along this route in GWR days, when it connected Ruabon to Barmouth.* ROBIN JONES

One of the strangest steam locomotive movements ever seen on a British railway: the steam power bogie being taken for test runs on the Llangollen Railway without the railmotor body! ADRIAN KNOWLES

The boiler being lifted into the restored railmotor body. ADRIAN KNOWLES

Auto trains were more flexible in operation and easier to maintain. The first GWR steam railmotor was withdrawn in 1914 and the last in 1935.

Steam railmotor No. 93 was built at Swindon Works in 1908 and was allocated to Bristol, Croes Newydd, Chalford, Gloucester, Stourbridge, Taunton and Yatton.

It was withdrawn in November 1934 and while its steam bogie was removed and scrapped, its body was converted into auto trailer No. 212. That ran in passenger service until May 1956, when it was converted into a British Railways work study coach and ended up as an office in Birmingham. Bought for preservation by the Great Western Society in 1970, it was all that remained of the GWR's once-proud railmotor fleet.

Meanwhile, in 1933, the GWR returned to the all-in-one concept with the introduction of the first of a hugely-successful successful series of diesel railcars, which, broadly speaking, paved the way for the first generation British Railways diesel railcars and multiple units of the 1950s, luxury trains like the Blue Pullman and later the InterCity 125 High Speed Trains, plus many other modern DMUs.

In 1988, the GWS officially launched a project to rebuild the auto trailer into its original form as steam railmotor No. 93.

The first landmark came in November 2000 when the main frame for the brand new power bogie unit was erected at Tyseley Locomotive Works under the supervision of engineer Bob Meanley. Elsewhere, new driving wheels and cylinder blocks were cast and machined and other components made, and in 2003 a rolling chassis emerged.

Israel Newton of Bradford built a new boiler, and the bogie and boiler were moved to Didcot in March 2008 pending the forging and machining all the remaining components.

In January 2009 the assembly was moved to the Llangollen Railway engineering workshops to be installed in the underframe of the coach body, which had been earlier sent there for restoration with the aid of a £768,500 Heritage Lottery Fund grant also awarded for the restoration of trailer car No. 92.

On 17 November 2010, the power bogie, looking every bit like a pioneer locomotive from the early days of steam, ran on its own up and down the Llangollen Railway and was found to work perfectly. Six days later, it was united with the body – and 75 years on, a GWR steam railmotor was reborn.

In the first instance, No. 93 was painted in the largely-forgotten previous GWR coach livery of 1912-22, crimson lake lined in gold with a white roof.

It finally entered traffic on Monday 21 March, carrying a party of project supporters from Llangollen to Carrog and back, before taking part in four days of enthusiast photo charters on the railway. The standard of finish both outside and inside, where even the finest details had been replicated, had to be seen to be believed. It was nothing less than a living, breathing, working time capsule of Edwardian train travel, and as such it is of immense historical importance.

Returned to Didcot, it ran there for the first time on 29 April, and was officially launched into traffic on 28 May by Adrian Shooter, chairman of main line operator Chiltern Railways, who brought along his newest DMU, a Class 172 Turbostar, delivered just two days before and never used by passengers. A replica of the GWR railmotor shed at Southall was opened the same day.

On Saturday 11 June, the railmotor, the only one of its kind running in Britain today, and therefore the embodiment of the great missing link between the steam and modern traction era, lined up at Didcot alongside the most famous new build locomotive of them all to date – No. 60163 *Tornado*.

*The full story of the groundbreaking railmotor project is the subject of companion volume Railmotor: The Steam Engine that Rewrote Railway History, *also published by Halsgrove.*

The railmotor is unique amongst new-build schemes in that the project included an exact replica of its original shed too! The railmotor shed at Didcot is based on the original at Southall. FRANK DUMBLETON/GWS

CHAPTER NINETEEN

REMEMBERING *THE UNKNOWN WARRIOR*

ONE OF THE FASTEST-DEVELOPING new-build projects, both it terms of public support and completion of major and minor components, is the scheme to build a new LMS Patriot 4-6-0.

Not only will the building of the locomotive fill a huge gap in preservation, but, uniquely, will also become the National Memorial Engine, a steam 'version' of the Cenotaph. Endorsed by the Royal British Legion, it will remember those who gave their lives in two world wars and subsequent conflicts, and accordingly, will be numbered and named 45551 *The Unknown Warrior*.

The scheme was the brainchild of David Bradshaw of the Great Western Society, who has played a significant part in Didcot's new-build *County of Glamorgan* project. Back in 2006, he saw that LMS preservation had missed out by not having a Barry scrapyard equivalent and had therefore lost more types than the GWR and Southern Railway. Furthermore, there was no LMS new-build project in existence, and one would in theory attract widespread support from followers of the company's heritage.

The three-cylinder LMS Patriot class was introduced towards the end of Sir Henry Fowler's reign as Chief Mechanical Engineer from 1925-32.

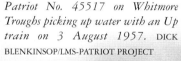

Patriot No. 45517 on Whitmore Troughs picking up water with an Up train on 3 August 1957. DICK BLENKINSOP/LMS-PATRIOT PROJECT

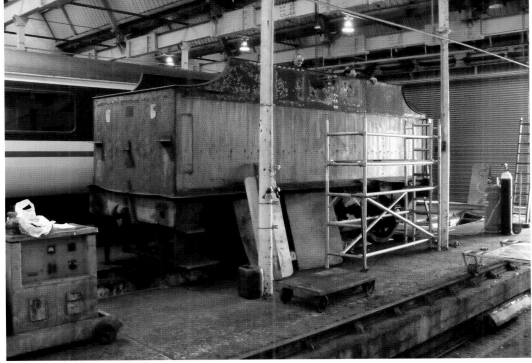

The Fowler tender for The Unknown Warrior *being dismantled at Barry. The first stage was the removal of the badly-corroded tender tank.* OAKWOOD VISUALS

The class was presented as a rebuild of Bowen-Cook's large-boilered Claughton 4-6-0s; indeed, the first two were produced from the remains of two Claughtons that had been badly damaged in accidents.

However, the Patriots, as they were known after 1937, had more in common with the Royal Scot, having a very similar chassis combined with the smaller G91/2S boiler as used on the rebuilt Claughtons. They were also known as 'Baby Scots' as a result.

A total of 57 were planned, but the last five were built with Taper boilers and became the first of the Jubilees.

All the Patriots were painted out in LMS crimson lake livery with pale yellow and black lining when first built, but after 1946 most were painted out in LMS lined black with straw and maroon lining. All of them were later reliveried in British Railways standard Brunswick green with orange and black.

Highly successful, the Patriots covered around 1.3 million miles each. They were all withdrawn in 1960-62 and scrapped, the standard gauge preservation movement having yet to become firmly established. The last two withdrawn were Nos. 45543 and 45550.

The LMS-Patriot Project has the mission statement to build a new Patriot to the original Sir Henry Fowler parallel boiler design, and capable of running over the national network.

The project was officially launched in April 2008 at the Llangollen Railway's spring steam gala. Assembly of *The Unknown Warrior* began in 2009 led by Dave Owen, Chief Mechanical Engineer at the Llangollen Railway's works.

In March that year, the frame plates for the new Patriot were cut by Corus Steel at Cradley Heath

Eddie Mocroft, master pattern maker at Boro Foundry in Lye, studies drawings for The Unknown Warrior's *axleboxes and frame stretchers.* LMS-PATRIOT PROJECT

in the West Midlands. The plates were taken to the aforementioned Boro Foundry in nearby Lye for drilling and machining, before being delivered to the Llangollen Railway where assembly of the locomotive is taking place.

Barry scrapyard again played its part. Along with the Barry Ten pool of scrap locomotives was an original Fowler tender. After it was acquired from the Vale of Glamorgan Council, the restoration of its chassis began at Cambrian Transport's Barry Railway Centre in November 2010, and a brand new tender body will be built.

Main line running would require the locomotive to be built to a height of 13ft – 2½in less than the original design.

The cost breakdown for the new Patriot has been estimated at £48,000 for the frames, £54,000 for the cylinders, £150,000 for the driving wheelsets, £70,000 for cab fittings and pipework, £30,000 for the tender refurbishment, and the biggest component of all, the boiler, was costed at £500,000. It is expected that the locomotive will overall cost in the region of £1.5-million.

The first driving wheel for *The Unknown Warrior* was cast at Boro Foundry on 13 September 2010, after readers of *Heritage Railway* magazine raised £60,000 to pay for all six to be cast.

Steve Blackburn, Patriot project quality and engineering director, Kevin West, project draughtsman; Rob Le Chevalier, workshop manager at the South Devon Railway, and project chairman David Bradshaw are seen with the fourth driving wheel cast at Boro Foundry in December 2010.
LMS-PATRIOT PROJECT

Above from left to right: *The smoke deflectors were sponsored by Patriot project member David Collins and were fabricated by John Whiteman engineering of Long Eaton under the supervision of project supporter Neil Kinsey who has overseen their construction; One of the machined Patriot driving wheels at Boro Foundry.* LMS-PATRIOT PROJECT; *The pony truck wheelset provided from a Stanier 8F reimported from Turkey.* LMS-PATRIOT PROJECT

Left: *Pouring the metal for the new wheels at Boro Foundry.* ROBIN JONES

Top right: *The dragbox for* The Unknown Warrior *was completed during December 2010 at the Llangollen Railway works where coded welder Ian Massey welded the pre-cut sections together.* ANDREW LAWS/LMS-PATRIOT PROJECT

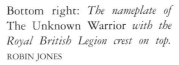

Bottom right: *The nameplate of* The Unknown Warrior *with the Royal British Legion crest on top.* ROBIN JONES

Artist Colin Wright paints The Unknown Warrior *on shed at Llangollen. A limited edition print was produced to raise funds for No. 45551.* JOHN HASTINGS-THOMSON/ LMS-PATRIOT PROJECT

The pattern for the driving wheels was loaned by Tyseley's chief engineer Bob Meanley. It had already been used to cast two new driving wheels for Jubilee 4-6-0 No. 45699 *Galatea*.

The pouring of the molten steel for the first wheel took only 90 seconds. After cooling for two days the new casting was revealed and was later shotblasted and machined, reducing the weight of the finished wheel.

All six were cast by January 2011. The fitting of the tyres, crank axle, plain axles and crank pins was contracted to the South Devon Railway.

On 19 November 210, the project announced that pop mogul Pete Waterman's LNWR Heritage Ltd at Crewe had been chosen as the preferred builder of the boiler for No. 45551. The all-new boiler will be built in the traditional way, with a copper firebox, riveted seams and screwed stays.

LNWR Heritage Ltd was elected as it has the technical capability and has already built new copper fireboxes at Crewe, including the one for LNER B1 4-6-0 No. 61264 owned by the Thompson B1 Locomotive Trust, and the spare A4 boiler For LNER Pacific No. 60019 *Bittern*.

The new Patriot boiler will be the first traditionally built large steam boiler to be constructed in the UK for a standard gauge main line steam locomotive since 1960.

In January 2011, a set of genuine LMS buffers of the type fitted to Patriots were acquired from a rail-mounted crane that was being scrapped at the Great Central Railway (Nottingham). At least three of the buffers are stamped LMS, with 1930s dates. The diesel-electric crane was built at Derby Works in 1947 and fitted with a set of buffers from an LMS locomotive that had been scrapped there.

A further boost came in June 2011 with the offer of an appropriate bogie wheelset from the Churchill 8F Locomotive Group, which overhauled repatriated former Turkish Railways Stanier 8F No. 45160 at the Gloucestershire Warwickshire Railway. The Patriot team already had a bogie wheelset from Barry Ten Storier 8F No. 48518, which had donated its boiler to the new Country project. So with all the wheels obtained, a rolling chassis by 2012 was looking likely. The LMS-Patriot Project has set a target date of 2018 for completion of No. 45551, to coincide with the 100th anniversary of the signing of the Armistice which brought about an end to the Great War, but again, funds from supporters and well-wishers are paramount. For me, there is little doubt that when it finally runs, it will be a tremendous source of pride not just for the railway preservation movement but for the country in general.

CHAPTER TWENTY
THE RETURN OF *LEW* AND *LYN*

MANY ARE THE LEGENDS that have grown around the Lynton & Barnstaple Railway, which opened as an independent 19½-mile 1ft 11½in gauge railway in May 1898 and was closed by subsequent owner the Southern Railway in September 1935.

Not least of all the stories surrounds the fate of *Lew*, its fifth locomotive, a Manning Wardle 2-6-2T bought by the Southern Railway in 1925.

While the other four locomotives, Manning Wardle 2-6-2Ts *Exe*, *Taw* and *Yeo*, and Baldwin 2-42 *Lyn*, were sold for scrap after closure, *Lew* was used by the contractors dismantling the railway before being sold for use in South America. In September 1936, *Lew* was loaded onto the *SS Sabor* destined for Recife (then Pernambuco) in Brazil.

Nothing has been heard of *Lew* again, leading to multiple theories about its fate. With shipping records destroyed in World War Two, nobody knows exactly where it ended up, whether it was

Officially, Lyd *is not a replica of* Lew, *but the subtle arrangement of project engineers' names on the Boston Lodge works plate indicates its true legacy.* ROBIN JONES

Lyd, *in mock BR livery, double heads with new-build single Fairlie* Taliesin *on the Ffestiniog Railway in early 2011.* ANDREW THOMAS/FR

Right: *New-build Manning Wardle 2-6-2T* Lyd *'returns' to the Lynton & Barnstaple Railway in September 2010. It is carrying a wreath, recalling the famous floral tribute left when the line closed, 'perchance it is not dead but merely sleepeth.'* TONY NICHOLSON

Above: Lew, *then just a year old, and* Taw *double head out of Barnstaple in 1926.* LBR

Below: *Built by the Baldwin Locomotive works in Philadelphia, the original* Lyn *was imported to Britain for use on the Lynton & Barnstaple Railway.* LBR

The cab for the new Lyn *and a wheel pattern displayed at Woody Bay.* ROBIN JONES

Far right: Freelance *new-build 0-4-0T* Emmet *relaunched steam services on the Lynton & Barnstaple Railway in 2004.* ROBIN JONES

The first wheels for Lyn *being cast in Sheffield on 14 April 2011.* TREFOIL

scrapped in 1957, as once reported, or simply left to rust away in the jungle as there was no scrap metal trade in Brazil at the time.

It has since become the holy grail of railway preservation, with attempts made by both British and Us enthusiasts to locate it in South America, or discover its true fate, but all so far in vain.

In 1979, the Lynton & Barnstaple Railway Association was formed with the aim of rebuilding the line from scratch, and in 1995 bought Woody Bay station as its headquarters. A short section of railway reopened to passengers in 2004, subsequently extended to nearly a mile in 2006, with steam and diesel-hauled trains running between Woody Bay and a temporary western terminus at Killington Lane short of Parracombe, the line's next goal.

The first steam locomotive to run at Woody Bay was *Emmet*, a freelance 0-4-0T built by Jim Haylock, owner of the Moors Valley Railway in Dorset.

While members rebuilt original carriages which had been retrieved from private use, as a stop-gap measure, a series of carriages from the railway at Thorpe Park theme park in Surrey were pressed into service in original L&B livery. However, no original and therefore authentic steam locomotives were available, so members realised they would have to build their own.

A set of frames for a replica of *Yeo* were built by Winson Engineering around 2000, and these are still in storage, awaiting further funds to continue the construction.

What reduced much of the impetus to proceed with the project was not only the cost of rebuilding the L&B itself, but the fact that the Ffestiniog Railway was building a new Manning Wardle 2-6-2T closely based on *Lew* at its Boston Lodge Works.

The locomotive, named *Lyd* after the L&B policy of choosing names of Devon rivers with three letters, first moved under its own steam at Boston Lodge on 5 August 2010 as the culmination of a 15-year project which was undertaken in fits and starts as money and resources became available.

After running-in trials, *Lyd* visited project supporter the Launceston Steam Railway in September that year before moving on to where else but the L&B. Thousands packed the little line's autumn gala to see the 'new *Lew*' haul former L&B coach No, 15 and Ffestiniog Railway observation car No. 102, which had been based on an L&B design. Both had been loaned for the occasion by Ffestiniog general manager Paul Lewin to run behind *Lyd* for the big occasion.

Although externally similar to *Lew*, *Lyd* has several modern design and construction techniques to improve overall efficiency.

Visitors to Woody Bay during the gala would have also seen the cab of another new-build locomotive taking shape, that of a replica of the Baldwin *Lyn*. Like the original, it was constructed out of American ash.

In 2008, L&B revivalists formed the 762 Club, taking its name from the original *Lyn's* Southern Railway number. The idea was that 350 supporters would each buy a share for £762 and raise the £266,700 needed to build the locomotive.

Sufficient numbers took up the share offer for a serious start to be made. A contract for a new all-welded boiler was awarded to Bennett Boilers of Highbridge in Somerset, and although based on the original dimensions will feature many improvements in detail. Computer modelling has confirmed that the new *Lyn* will be a more powerful and efficient engine than its prototype.

The contract for the erection of the finished locomotive was awarded to Alan Keef Ltd in Ross-on-Wye, and on 14 April, the first two of eight wheels were cast at the Trefoil Steel Company plant in Tinsley, Sheffield, and later machined. Such has been the progress on the new *Lyn* that a steaming towards the end of 2012 was looking possible.

Meanwhile, in December 2010, *Lyd* was painted in early 1950s British Railways lined black livery with the number 30190, showing what might have been had the line not closed in 1935. In August 2011, it was taken into the paint shop at Boston Lodge to be turned out in the livery everyone wanted to see – Southern Railway lined Maunsell green, carried by *Lew* on the L&B, and numbered 190.

Incidentally, a full-size 2ft Manning Wardle-style 2-6-2T, *Green Breeze*, loosely based on the L&B types was built by Winson Engineering of Daventry in 1998 for the Usui Pass Museum near Tokyo and exported in 1998. It was described as combination of the original design and later modifications.

Lyd's *first driving and pony truck wheels ready for machining.* ROBIN JONES

Replica Lynton & Barnstaple Manning Wardle 2-6-2T Lyd *was finally rolled out in Southern Railway green livery at Boston Lodge Works on 7 September.* ANDREW THOMAS

CHAPTER TWENTY ONE
TWO NEW B17S
ARE BETTER THAN ONE

AS THE *TORNADO* PROJECT neared its final stages in 2008, a group aiming to plug not one but two more gaps in LNER locomotive heritage broke cover.

The North British Locomotive Group, better known for its repatriation of Glasgow-built locomotives from South Africa, finally announced a scheme to build not one but two new B17 4-6-0 'Sandringhams' after it had been simmering behind closed doors for a decade.

One of the planned B17s will be built to operational standard, for use on both the main line and heritage railways.

The other will be a non-working example for exhibition for static display at museums.

One of the locomotives will carry the name *Sandringham* after the first member of the class, while

LNER B17 4-6-0 No 2806 Audley End at Westerfield station, the junction for Felixstowe on the Ipswich-Lowestoft line. GER SOCIETY/ PHOTOMATIC

the other will recreate one of the very similar B17 'Footballers' which were named after football clubs in regions served by the LNER.

One GER-type tender and one LNER tender would be provided, allowing authentic exchanges between the pair. Therefore, either a 'Sandringham' or a 'Footballer' would be available for work at any one time while the other engine remained on display.

When completed, the display engine will be sited at an appropriate East Anglian location.

The group already had a B1 tender, which had been languishing in a siding at Sheringham station on the North Norfolk Railway.

Like the Peppercorn A1 Pacific and the LMS Patriot, the 'Sandringham' has been high on the public 'wish list' of fabled locomotives to be recreated.

The B17s date back to the General Strike of 1926, when a shortage of quality coal led to failures of ageing pre-Grouping locomotives on the LNER, and its Great Eastern district in particular.

There was also a shortage of express passenger locomotives to cope with heavier workloads and new vacuum-braked coaches, and because of the GER loading gauge restrictions, it was not possible to switch suitable engine types from other parts of the LNER system.

LNER management told their Chief Mechanical Engineer to produce a new 4-6-0 design to complement the existing B12s. The job was delegated to the North British Locomotive Company.

In February 1928, the LNER accepted a design for a locomotive with an 18-ton axle loading, even though it would restrict the route availability to a set number of GER main lines.

The design adopted many features from a North British batch of LNER A1 Pacifics built in 1924, including the cab, cylinders, and motion, while the boiler design was based on the K3 2-6-0 and O2 2-8-0 designs.

Ten were ordered, the first B17 being delivered on 30 November 1928. Darlington turned out 52 between 1930-36, with Robert Stephenson adding a final batch of 11 in 1937, making a total of 73.

No. 2800, *Sandringham*, began a sequence of B17s named after English country houses, while No. 2848 *Arsenal* was the first in the line named after football clubs.

The B17s proved popular on the London to Cambridge route, but less so on the line to Ipswich because of steeper

The first of the cabs for the new B17s was fabricated in 2008. NBLPS

A headboard from one of the famous named trains hauled by B17s. ROBIN JONES

Patterns for smaller components of the new B17s on display at Barrow Hill in September 2008. ROBIN JONES

gradients. Eventually they worked the cross-country service from Ipswich to Manchester and East Anglia's heavy boat trains.

The first 'Sandringham' to be withdrawn was No. 61604 *Elveden* in 1953, and the majority of the class were taken out of service in 1958-59.

The last survivor, No. 61668 *Bradford City*, was scrapped at Stratford in September 1960, before the preservation movement was able to address the issue. When the locomotives were scrapped, many of the football nameplates were given to the clubs.

The loss of all the 'Sandringhams' and 'Footballers', as later engines in the class became known, was greatly mourned by enthusiasts of the time and left a huge void in the LNER classes available for preservation.

Within a short time of the appeal being launched, a cab was built. The group subsequently bought a set of original GER tender frames from the Midland & Great Northern Joint Railway Society, complete with wheels and axleboxes, some of which actually have B17 cast on them. Therefore the group now has the basis of both the LNER and GER tenders that are required to build both types of B17.

The project received a major blow with the death of its project engineer Kim Malyon, who had overseen the rebuilding of many of today's steam locomotives, at the age of 63 on 27 April 2010.

However, members vowed to continue with the project, which has to raise a substantial seven-figure sum if it is to achieve its very laudable aims.

In early 2011, the B17 Steam Locomotive Trust was formed to take over the construction of the new locomotives from the Sandringham Locomotive Company, which had previously been set up to oversee the project.

CHAPTER TWENTY TWO
A NEW HOLDEN F5 TANK

A RARE EXAMPLE OF A London Underground line to close is the Central Line's 6½-mile former Great Eastern Railway branch from Epping to Chipping Ongar, which was electrified as recently as 1957 and which lost its passenger services due to low uptake on 30 September 1994. Since then, the line has been the subject of various attempts to reopen it firstly as a commuter line, and at present as a heritage railway.

Shortly after it closed, the Ongar Railway Preservation Society was formed to take over the line, but the Government instead awarded it to a private company, Pilot Developments, a move which sparked great controversy amongst enthusiasts, especially when the promised commuter services failed to start.

Undeterred, ORPS members bided their time, while planning for a day when they might yet take over the redundant route. Looking at the progress being made on *Tornado*, in 2001 several of them decided to build a replica of a GER F5 2-4-2 tank engine, a type which had formed the mainstay of services on the branch prior to electrification.

The original F5s were designed by GER Locomotive Superintendent James Holden as a development of his predecessor William Worsdell's M15 2-4-2Ts. At first, the M15s were modified into F5s by fitting Stephenson valve gear as a major improvement over the poorly-performing Joys value gear. A second batch, the P55s was built new to this design between 1903-9, and altogether a total of 160 engines were built at Stratford Works.

Stephen Dewar Holden followed in the footsteps of his father in 1908 and built a batch of 20 larger versions of the M15 with a boiler of higher pressure and increased water and coal capacity, which raised the overall weight by 3 tons. Twenty of these engines were built by the GER and could be distinguished by the side cab windows which later became LNER class F6. Some P55 s were rebuilt with the higher-pressure boilers from 1911-20 and became classified as M15R. After the Grouping in 1923, classes M15/M15R became LNER F4 and F5 respectively.

At nationalisation, 37 F4s and all 30 F5s passed into BR

Great Eastern Railway F5 2-4-2 tank No 67202 at Epping shed in 1950, still providing sterling service in the early days of British Railways.
EPPING ONGAR RAILWAY SOCIETY

The new chimney for the Holden F5.
HSLT

ownership and all were given the prefix '6' to their number. In 1949, seven F5s were fitted with vacuum push-pull gear: of these, Nos. 67193, 67200, 67202, 6723 and 67213 were based at Epping to work the Ongar shuttle. No. 67218 later joined Nos 67200 and 67212 for the last scheduled steam trains on the branch on 16 November 1957.

OPRS pioneer members Graham Rowland, Stephen Cooper and Ian Strugnall saw that the F5 would not only be the most suitable to work over a revived Ongar branch but also on heritage railways anywhere, weighing just 16 tons. No major modifications were made to the class and the new engine could run in GER blue and grey liveries, LNER, BR black, with or without push-pull gear and with or without trip cocks. Coal oil could be used to authentically fire the engine as Holden experimented with oil burning on some locomotives including M5 No. 650.

The National Railway Museum held a huge amount of drawings, including some of the F4/F5

The smokebox and bufferbeam of the new F5, No. 67218. The door handles and dart are also in place and lock against the crossbar temporarily bolted to the door plate of the smokebox. HSLT

The bunker being built at Hunwicks in Halstead, Essex, in March 2010. HSLT

Pictured in 2005 is the non-driving wheel pattern and core box with, from left to right, Graham Rowland (Holden F5 Steam Locomotive Trust), Dave Harriman (South Lincs Patterns), John Hazlehurst (pattern maker, South Lincs Patterns) and Steve Cooper (Holden F5 Steam Locomotive Trust). HSL

on microfiche.

It was decided to number the new F5 67218. To start the project, a 30A Stratford shed plate was bought from Procast of Cleckheaton, following by the sourcing of various minor components. In June 2002 the Holden Steam Locomotive Trust was granted charitable status, and in autumn 2003 it located a suitable workshop at Ovington in North Essex.

The trust was granted corporate membership of the Heritage Railway Association in March 2004.

During 2004 and 2005, the valences and buffer beams were completed and assembled, and patterns were made for the non driving wheels.

Over the years, steady progress has been made, with the mainframe, the first major component, due to be cut in 2011.

CHAPTER TWENTY THREE
BRINGING BACK *BLYTH* TO SOUTHWOLD

The frames for the new Sharp Stewart 2-4-0T. SRS

IN 1929, IT VERY NEARLY BECAME Britain's first heritage railway, 22 years before volunteers began running the Talyllyn. However, it was not to be, and the much-lampooned Southwold Railway, which had opened 50 years before passed into history. Indeed, it is one of the great legendary British narrow gauge lines still to be revived at least in part, despite several attempts.

After the closed on 11 April 1929, two attempts to revive it came to nothing. One involved relaying the 3ft gauge track (common in Ireland and the Isle of Man but rare on the British mainland) to standard gauge and extending it to meet the Mid-Suffolk Light Railway, while the other would have kept the gauge, but special wagons on which standard gauge wagons could be carried would be introduced, increasing freight revenue, with petrol railcars brought in for passengers. Sadly, it was lifted in 1941 as scrap for the war effort, and the locomotive and most of the stock scrapped.

In 2002, the Southwold Railway Society, which was formed eight years earlier, began drawing up plans for a full-blown revival.

An initial proposal to reopen the line along the original route was dropped following a public consultation process. The society, which runs its own shop at 27 High Street, Southwold, then drew

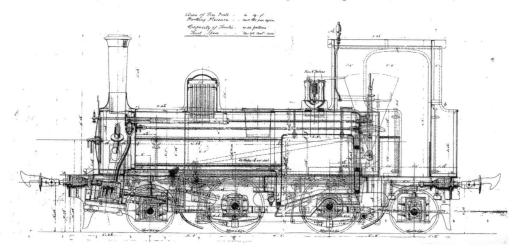

The engineering drawings for the full-size replica of Blyth. SRS

up a radical scheme to rebuild the railway, but using a new route west of Blyth, following the northern bank of the river estuary rather than the south.

However, following public protests, the society's planning application for a new line was rejected by Suffolk Coastal and Waveney district councils in 2007.

Two years later, however, the Southwold Railway Trust won permission to build a steam theme park with a 2ft gauge demonstration railway on the site of a car spares outlet and waste disposal site in Blyth Road on the edge of the resort.

Since then, that idea has been placed on the back burner, with members concentrating on a scheme to relay 1¼ miles of the original line at Wenhaston. Central to the project is the building of a replica of one of the original Sharp Stewart 2-4-0Ts of 1879, No. 3 *Blyth*. In early 2010, the frames of the £120,000 replica, made by Aldeburgh metalworkers Sam and Dennis Pegg, and housed in a local builder's shed, were unveiled, at the launch of a buy-a-share scheme to raise the rest of the necessary finance. Inside the shed, two 15ft lengths of original 30lb rail on sleepers were installed to support the construction.

The society has launched the '2-4-0 Club' to generate funds by seeking sponsorship in £240 units relating to 172 specific components including 58 boiler tubes. One idea was to commemorate those who worked on the railway first time round by naming tubes after them.

It is planned to use volunteer labour to assemble the new *Blyth* and involve local schools and colleges in its construction.

A Sharp Stewart 2-4-0T heads a mixed Southwold Railway train at Blythburgh station in the early twentieth century. SRS

CHAPTER TWENTY FOUR

THE GWR ENGINE THAT NEVER WAS, AND OTHER CONVERSIONS

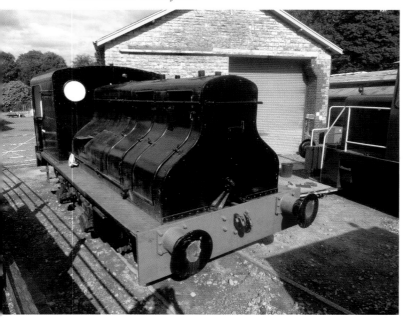

AFTER THE WEST SOMERSET RAILWAY had acquired an unrestored Barry hulk, 1934-built GWR prairie tank No. 5193, from the defunct Steamport museum at Southport rather than restore "yet another" 2-6-2T, a type generously represented in preservation, it was decided to turn it into a tender locomotive.

The railway worked out that by adding a tender and turning the prairie into a 2-6-0, it would create a locomotive similar to the GWR 4300 and 9300 class types which regularly worked over it during the steam era, only two of which made it into preservation.

While the finished looks at a glance to be exactly like a GWR mogul, with outside steam pipes, lever reverse and flanged motion bracket, it is a new class of locomotive – a type which was considered on several occasion by the GWR but which never even reached the detailed design stage.

Both Churchward and Collett considered building a small-boilered mogul as lighter version of the 4300 and 9300 classes, but the weight saving was not considered sufficient to take the idea further.

However, many decades later West Somerset officials decided that not only would a 'new' type of GWR mogul be in line with the mission statement of recreating the Minehead branch as it was in the days of steam, but popular with the general public who prefer to see tender engines on services. While the chassis forward of the cab is identical to a traditional GWR mogul, the standard No 2. boiler of the large prairie is 5½in smaller and has lower pitch than the No. 4 boiler fitted to the 4300s. Other minor detail changes from the original moguls include the position of the curve on the front footplate, the forward-facing flange on the motion plate, the spring type and the compensating beam type.

Also, while the cab design will have the larger side windows of the 9300s, lever reverse follows the format of the 4300 so as to offer the greatest level of crew protection.

The conversion was carried out in a way that the locomotive could

be reconverted to a large prairie in the future, if the demand arose, so an historic locomotive would not be lost. Furthermore, the cost of building the mogul was found to be not much more than restoring it as a 5101 class prairie, of which 10 survive into preservation.

However, it is not labelled as a new GWR type, but a West Somerset Railway class.

Unveiled in 2004, the new mogul, No. 9351 – an anagram of the prairie tank's number – proved that the GWR tradition of innovation in locomotive design is still very much alive on its former territory.

The West Somerset is home to one of the sole surviving Somerset & Dorset Joint Railway locomotives, 7F 2-8-0 No. 88, its sister, No. 53809, being based at the Midland Railway-Butterley. However, a smaller group elsewhere in the county is progressing a modest conversion scheme to create a third S&D engine.

A group of members of the Somerset & Dorset Railway Heritage Trust at Midsomer Norton station are converting former Croydon Gas Works Sentinel 0-4-0VBT No. 7109 of 1927 *Joyce* into one of its S&D sister locomotives Nos. 101 or 102.

Although No. 7109 never ran on the S&D, there is a strong link between it and the low-bodied pair which, with their unmistakable bell-shaped smokebox and boiler cladding, were needed to haul coal trains below Radstock's Tyning Bridge, which had only a 10ft 10in clearance.

Following the success of trials of No. 7109 at Newton Heath carriage works prior to delivery to the gas works, the LMS ordered three production examples with slight modifications in 1929, and two were sent to the S&D.

They were later renumbered by the LMS as 7190 and 7191 and following nationalisation became BR Nos. 47190 and 47191.

Apart from the highly distinctive shape, an odd feature about this type of Sentinel was the two chimneys. Each pair of cylinders was connected to a separate smokebox.

No. 47191 was withdrawn in 1959 and the demolition of the bridge the following year rendered its sister locomotive redundant and it too was scrapped.

To convert *Joyce* into one of its successors off the Shrewsbury production line, all that was needed was for its cab to be lowered and modified.

Joyce was named after the daughter of the gas company chairman, a Mr Sandeman, and arrived there in January 1928. It worked until the late 1950s when lorry transport began to replace the movement of coal by rail within the gas works.

The preservation sector has several examples of industrial locomotives being cosmetically converted to appear as Thomas the Tank Engine characters. At the Mid-Hants Railway, two Hunslet Austerity saddle tanks met this fate.

No. 3781 of 1954 was converted into a side tank as 'Thomas No. 1', while No. 2890 of 1943 was stripped of its tanks, given a tender and turned into the Reverend Wilbert Awdry's character *Douglas*. The aim of both conversions was, of course, to boost Thomas events, which have been a vital sources of income for the railway and others.

Two converted Austerity saddle tanks line up as Thomas characters at the Mid-Hants Railway. MHR

CHAPTER TWENTY FIVE
IT'S A SMALL WORLD

SO FAR IN THIS BOOK we have looked mainly at the building of replica locomotives to fill a gap in the nation's heritage fleet or a special local need.

At the same time, commercial steam railway locomotive building has continued unabated in Britain, with small firms – perhaps the modern-day equivalent of the likes of Peckett, Avonside and Manning Wardle – supplying ready-to-run engines to theme park railways, seaside and miniature

One of Britain's newest steam locomotives is the Wells & Walsingham Light Railway's second Garratt, Norfolk Heroine, *which entered service in 2011.* ROBIN JONES

Quarry Hunslet-style locomotive Dame Ann *was built by the Exmoor Steam Railway for export to the USA.* EXMOOR

The Wells & Walsingham Light Railway's articulated Beyer Garratt Norfolk Hero. BRIAN SHARPE

lines and private systems, some of which are rarely if ever open to the general public.

Near Bratton Fleming in North Devon, the 12¼in gauge Exmoor Steam Railway at Cape of Good Hope Farm was established by the Stirland family in 1990 as a public attraction, after 20 years in the plant hire business.

As ready-made locomotives were scarce and expensive, Trevor Stirland decided to use their expertise in welding and machining to build their own. They performed so successfully that orders came in from private customers, and in 2001 the decision was taken to cease public operation of the on-site railway but to retain it as a test track, to which end an additional half mile on a gradient of 1-in-28 was brought into use in 2009.

The firm has now built no fewer than 50 locomotives in gauges of 7¼in, 10¼in, 12¼in and 15in – and one 2ft gauge Quarry Hunslet type, which predated the Statford Barn examples, for a railway in Alabama. They are all individually designed for customers by the Stirland family.

The entire fleet of four steam engines on the 12¼in gauge Exbury Gardens Railway in Hampshire was built by Exmoor. A woman disguised by a grey raincoat and a headscarf who accepted a cab ride in one of them, newly-built 2-6-2 *Mariloo*, on 3 May 2008 turned out to be none other than HM The Queen. As astonished onlookers gazed in wonder, she sat in the fireman's seat alongside the gardens' owner, 80-year-old banker Leopold de Rothschild, a personal friend, as he drove *Mariloo*.

Just outside Ross-on-Wye in Herefordshire is Alan Keef Limited, founded by chairman Alan Keef in 1968. His son, Patrick Keef is managing director and his daughter, Alice Basey, is chief design engineer. The company employs eight skilled craftsmen in its factory, three members of the management support team in the offices and a four-man track gang which undertakes the on-site construction and maintenance of trackwork.

The firm has an excellent reputation throughout the 10¼in to 3ft 6in gauge railway industry as a supplier of quality modern railway equipment, replica historic railway equipment and as a restorer of historic equipment. Its work is regularly inspected and endorsed by HM Railway Inspectorate.

Exmoor Steam Railway-built Mariloo *with Union flags and lamps set in royal code for a visit by Prince Charles, who drove the locomotive in May 2011.* EXBURY

Not only does the firm supply to such traditional markets as mining, tunnelling, the peat industry, sugar and other plantations, but will provide complete railways, including the planning and construction of the track and the design and construction of locomotives, carriages and other rolling stock for miniature and narrow gauge lines. It has also designed and supplied replica locomotives and rolling stock to some of the major preserved railways and museums in the UK and Ireland.

At Ashley Heath in Dorset near the Hampshire boundary to the north of Bournemouth is the Moors Valley Railway. It is much more than a traditional 7¼in gauge railway, as its generous loading gauge permitting large rolling stock places it in the narrow gauge rather than miniature railway category. Indeed, it is more akin to a main line network.

Built on farmland, the railway boasts two signal boxes, track circuiting, a mixture of colour light and semaphore signals all linked by a lineside emergency telephone system. Infrastructure includes two stations, three gated level crossings, three footbridges, two tunnels and perhaps its main feature, a spiral.

Jim Haylock, who conceived and built the mile-long line first became seriously involved in locomotive design and construction when a member of the Malden Model Engineering Club, Thames Ditton. He was inspired when former Romney Hythe & Dymchurch Railway chief engineer, Roger Marsh built a 0-4-2T which he named *Tinkerbell*, and wanted one for his own garden railway.

Jim first opened a railway in a small theme park at Christchurch, where he began locomotive construction.

Operating with 0-4-2Ts No. 4 *Tinkerbell* and another Marsh engine, No. 3 *Talos*, work began building 4-6-0 No. 5 *Sapper* (rebuilt 1993), 0-4-4T No. 7 *Aelfred*, 0-6-2T *Medea* and a privately owned 2-4-0 tender engine, No. 1 *Sir Goss*.

When the site was sold for building development, the railway was moved to its present location, where it carries more than 100,000 passengers each year.

Since moving to its present location, the railway's workshop has turned out eight of its own engines ranging from 2-4-4T No. 9 *Jason*, built in 1989, to three 2-6-2s No. 10 *Offa*, No.11 *Zeus* and No. 12 *Pioneer*. Almost unique in the world of 7¼in gauge railways, No. 15 *William Rufus* was outshopped as a 2-4-0+0-4-2 Garratt in 1997. Building continues unabated. In summer 2011, two 0-4-02Ts were constructed for private owners.

It should be added that since 1999 five locomotives were built for private owner-drivers. These are 0-4-4-T No. 16 *Robert Fooks*, 0-4-4T No. 17 *Hartfield*, 4-6-2 No. 18 *Thor*, 2-8-0 No. 19 *Athelstan* and 0-4-2T No. 24 *Perseus*.

Not one but two new-build articulated Garratts can be found on the world's smallest public railway, the 4½-mile Wells & Walsingham Light Railway in Norfolk. The first, *Norfolk Hero*, was built in 1986, the second, *Norfolk Heroine* in 2010, both by engineer Neil Simkins.

Elsewhere in Norfolk, Bressingham Steam Museum unveiled what was then Britain's newest steam locomotive on 3 September 2010. A freelance 2ft 0-4-0, it had been designed and partially built by Bevan Braithwaite, chairman of the museum's trustees, and left to it when he died aged 68. It was named *Bevan* in his honour by his widow Vanda.

Mariloo speeding through Exbury Gardens with HM The Queen on board. JS BUNCH/EXBURY

One man not only built a 15in railway but the locomotives to run on it as well.

The founder of the Kirklees Light Railway, Brian Taylor, was a prolific model engineer building locomotives, traction engines and stationary engines in all sizes.

Commercial railways came when he opened the Shibden Park Miniature Railway in Halifax in 1984. For this 10¼in gauge railway he constructed a GNR Atlantic and a freelance 0-6-0ST *Ivor*.

Shibden whetted his appetite for a bigger line, and so he built the KLR on the trackbed of the former Lancashire & Yorkshire Shelley to Clayton West branch.

In 1987 he began construction of the first 15in gauge locomotive, a half-size Hunslet-style 2-6-2T named *Fox*, which steamed three years later.

Badger, a cross between Kerr Stuart Tattoo class and the North Wales Narrow Gauge Railway's Hunslet 0-6-4ST *Beddgelert*, followed in 1991.

Patrick Keef's 2ft gauge new-build vertical-boilered four-wheeler Taffy *based on a Victorian de Winton design in action on the Statfold Barn Railway.* ROBIN JONES

Clockwise from top left: *One of the more unusual locomotives built by Patrick Keef was this replica Listowel & Ballybunion Railway locomotive for a recreation of the legendry Lartigue monorail line in Ireland. Unlike the Hunslet originals, this one only looked like a steam engine, but for convenience had a diesel engine inside.* ALAN KEEF; *Outshopped in 1999 2-4-4T Hartfield is pictured in the Moors Valley Railway's Kingsmere loco yard.* CEDRIC JOHNS; *Fairbourne Railway's replica* Yeo, *built by the late David Curwen.* ROBIN JONES; *Styled on South African Railways locomotive design, 2-6-2 No 11 Zeus is one of three similar types built in the Moors Valley Railway workshop for heavy passenger traffic.* CEDRIC JOHNS

The 0-2-0 steam Monoloco. JOHN STRETTON

Hawk was truly different. Completed in 1998, it based on was a 2ft 3in gauge Kitson Meyer articulated 0-4-0+0-4-0 constructed by Barclay in 1903 for the Anglo Greek Magnesite Company in Chile. It is one of the most powerful 15in gauge locomotives in the world.

Owl was Brian's final locomotive (1999-2000) and also strangest. A Heisler with a V twin engine, it was based on an engraving of a proposed locomotive by Avonside in the 1920s. Its two cylinders drive Stephenson valve gear which through carden shafts drives two gear boxes on each power bogie. Brian passed away in 2009.

David Curwen, the first chief engineer on the volunteer-led Talyllyn Railway, was also a prolific steam builder, who began constructing locomotives in 1947 when his engineering firm, David Curwen Ltd, delivered a LNER Pacific to the Hilsea Lido Railway at Portsmouth and built a second at the same time.

In all he built 47 locomotives, steam and diesel, in gauges from 7¼in to 2ft gauge and all but one is still in existence. Two of his locomotives, scaled-down

Hive of industry: the Exmoor Steam Railway's production line. EXMOOR

Originally built as a 2-6-2 by Guest Engineering in 1964 with an internal diesel engine and called Tracey Jo, *it was later rebuilt as a steam engine and converted to a 2-6-4 in 1992 by Winson Engineering and is now No. 1* Wroxham Broad *in the Bure Valley Railway fleet.* BVR

David Curwen's scaled-down version of long-scrapped North Wales Narrow Gauge 0-6-4ST Beddgelert, *part of the Fairbourne Railway fleet.* FAIRBOURNE

replicas of *Beddgelert* and Lynton & Barnstaple Manning Wardle *Yeo*, run on the 12¼in gauge Fairbourne Railway today. He also built eight locomotives for Lord Braybrooke's Audley End Railway. Sadly, he died in 2011 at the age of 98.

Winson Engineering was a steam locomotive builder in Daventry in the 1990s. It built and overhauled both miniature and narrow gauge locomotives, several of which can be seen running on the 15in gauge Bure Valley Railway in Norfolk today.

In June 2001, Winson went into receivership and subsequently closed.

The Gartell Light Railway, a 2ft gauge line built on part of the trackbed on the Somerset & Dorset main line near Templecombe, has its own workshops, and also runs two steam locomotives, 0-4-2T *Mr G* and 0-4-0T *Jean*, built by the North Dorset locomotive works based in Shaftesbury.

Listing the private individuals who have engineered their own locomotives capable of hauling passenger trains on miniature and narrow gauge would occupy a volume in itself. However, one of the most unusual was the steam monoloco built by enthusiast Rich Morris, who previously owned the Gloddfa Ganol narrow gauge railway and mining centre at Blaenau Ffestiniog. Built by engineering company Century Millwrights on Platts Eyot, a small island in the River Thames, over two years, the world's only 0-2-0 tank engine made its public debut at the International Model Railway Exhibition at Kensington Olympia in December 1997. It now runs on a system at his private site in Blaenau Ffestiniog.

Clockwise from top left: *Brian Taylor's unusual Kitson Meyer articulated locomotive* Owl. KLR: *Fox, Brian Taylor's first locomotive for the Kirklees Light Railway.* STUART ROSS/KLR; *Alan Keef 15in gauge 2-6-2T* Lydia *built for the Perrygrove Railway in the Forest of Dean. This locomotive incorporates a number of "modern steam" features and is designed for low maintenance and operating costs.* ALAN KEEF; *Bunty, built for the Heatherslaw Light Railway, England's most northerly steam line, near Berwick-on-Tweed. This 2-6-0 tender engine was started in the 15in gauge railway's own workshop but completed by Alan Keef.* ALAN KEEF

CHAPTER TWENTY SIX

NEXT IN LINE

WITH THE PRINCIPLE, POTENTIAL and possibility of building a new steam locomotive of any size now established, and *Tornado* having blazed a media trail to show the general public just what can be achieved, more and more new schemes are being launched.

With *Tornado* now operating successfully on the main line, the thoughts of The A1 Steam Locomotive Trust inevitably started to turn to "what next"?

It has always been the desire of many members and supporters to tackle one of Sir Nigel Gresley's magnificent LNER P2 Mikados, the first of which, No. 2001 *Cock O' The North*, was completed at Doncaster Works in 1934, when it became the most powerful express passenger steam locomotive ever built for a British railway, designed to haul heavy trains from Edinburgh to Aberdeen.

Artists impression of No. 2001 Cock O' The North. A1SLT

No. 4700, the doyen of Churchward's 47XX mixed traffic 2-8-0 class of nine locomotives, in passenger action. GWS

The P2s' 2-8-2 wheel arrangement and 6ft 2in driving wheels enabled them to haul 600 ton trains on their own, replacing two older locomotives. However, they never lived up to their potential: the advent of the streamlined trains in the late 1930s and then the Second World War meant that the design was never fully developed and all six were rebuilt as class A2/2 Pacifics in 1943/44 by Gresley's successor Edward Thompson, effectively making the magnificent Mikados extinct. The rebuilt engines were scrapped in 1961.

Very importantly, it has around 70% commonality with *Tornado*, including the boiler, tender and many other detailed fittings.

The trust is conducting a feasibility study into the construction of a new Gresley P2, to be numbered 2007 as the next in the series. If it is decided that the trust can successfully and commercially build, certify and operate a P2, such a project will be launched. If not, then the trust will consider another locomotive to build: no metal for the P2 will be cut until the results of computer modelling are known and the trust sure that the design will be acceptable to Network Rail.

In much the same way that *Tornado* was constructed as the 50th A1 rather than a replica of an original member of the class, the proposed No. 2007 would be the seventh member of the P2 class, also allowing for improvements and variations in design to eliminate certain weaknesses. For instance,

GWR Churchward County 4-4-0 No. 3808 County Limerick, *built in 1906, passes Iver on 5 August 1929. It was withdrawn in 1931.*
GREAT WESTERN TRUST

unlike with the originals, it is proposed that No. 2007 will have roller bearings throughout.

However, a decision to closely follow the pattern set by *Cock O' The North* means that the locomotive will have the original semi-streamlining and rotary cam valve gear and will look, to all intents and purposes, like No. 2001.

Many of the patterns will be common to both *Tornado* and No. 2007 and therefore save much of expense, giving the trust a head start: indeed a spare cannon box already exists! It is also proposed that the tender will be identical to that used by *Tornado*, and braking will follow the design perfected during the construction of No. 60163, primary air brakes for locomotive and train with secondary vacuum brakes for working preserved stock. The electrical system will copy the system fitted to Tornado, although the original P2s did not have a Stones generator or electric lighting.

The trust also has the huge benefit of first-hand experience in having attained full main line certification of a new steam locomotive. It has estimated the cost of building No. 2007 at £5-million, making it Britain's most expensive new-build project to date.

Meanwhile, a separate group, the Doncaster P2 Locomotive Trust, formed in the late nineties, is also planning to build a new *Cock O' The North*, and in 2011 was examining quotes with regards to getting a set of main frame side members cut, after buying a set of electronic copies of the relevant drawings from the National Railway Museum. It is planned to build the new P2 in Doncaster, where the first *Cock O' The North* was originally constructed. In spring 2000, Great Western Society chairman Richard Croucher joined the project as a consultant.

Meanwhile, the GWS has by no means given up on its recycling of Barry Ten components. In July 2011, it announced the final green light for a long-mooted project to recreate a new 47XX 2-8-0, No. 4709. The last class introduced by Churchward, in 1919-21, only nine were built, and while they were intended for fast freight, they occasionally hauled passenger trains. The last was withdrawn in 1964 and none survived.

A GWS project team negotiated with the Vale of Glamorgan Council to obtain Barry Ten GWR prairie tank No. 4115 as a parts donor, providing three of the four necessary 5ft 8in driving wheel sets and the extension frame assembly, while another of the rusting hulks, GWR 2-8-0 No, 2861 would provide the outside-steam-pipe cylinder block which can be modified to suit the 4700, as well as the pony truck. The team already has the 4000-gallon tender which came with *Maindy Hall*.

Many components below the running plate of a third Barry Ten engine, GWR 2-8-0T No. 5227 are also common with the 47XX class, in particular the axleboxes and horns.

However, many other parts, including the No. 7 boiler, will have to be made new.

Extensive interest since the project was officially announced in spring 2010 has been backed by cash donations, combined with much behind-the-scenes preparatory work, leading to the final decision that it is feasible.

Preparations are being made to start physical work on the 47XX, beginning with the cutting of the frames.

All 'left over' Barry Ten components will be stored for use in further new-build schemes, the next in line after the 47XX being the Churchward County 4-4-0.

Lacking the glamour of their larger cousins the Saints, this class of 40 engines made a significant contribution to the efficient operation of the GWR over three decades and they were the first truly

The original No. 567 pictured when first outshopped from Gorton Works in January 1891. 567 GROUP

modern 4-4-0s produced in Britain, pre-dating the Southern Schools and LNER Hunts and Shires by almost 30 years.

They were Churchward's Edwardian engineering solution to the requirement for a locomotive of medium power output and provided a radically different approach to that of his predecessor William Dean who was responsible for the classical Victorian lines (though not the boilers) of the double framed 4-4-0s of the City, Armstrong, Atbara, Badminton and Flower classes.

The first appeared between May and October 1904 and were named after counties, with the first carrying the name *County of Middlesex*.

Withdrawal commenced in 1930 and all were scrapped by the end of 1933.

Under the aforementioned Three Counties Project plan, a new Churchward County 4-4-0 would use the No 4 boiler, frame stretchers, brake gear, lever reverser, eccentric sheave, cab grab handles, spring hangers, steps and vacuum cylinder from No. 5227; one 3ft 2in bogie wheelset, all four axleboxes and eight hornguides from No. 2861 and the remaining 3ft 2in bogie wheelset from No. 4115.

The Vale of Glamorgan Council has also provided the society with a suitable unrestored 3500-gallon spare tender from the Barry collection.

The patterns for the 6ft 8½in driving wheels and the cylinders are the same commissioned for the *Lady of Legend* Saint project.

The remaining components required are a full set of motion and a front bogie which would be made from new along with a new set of main frames.

Such a locomotive would fill a very obvious gap in the Great Western collection and would highlight the differences between Victorian and Edwardian design through a direct comparison with *City of Truro*. A Churchward County would also be an ideal size for use on heritage railways.

In 2009, the Swindon & Cricklade Railway launched a long-term project to build a replica of Midland and South Western Junction Railway Beyer Peacock 2-6-0 No. 16 of 1897.

No. 16 was built to a similar design to 70 locomotives delivered to the New South Wales Government Railway between 1881-85 and one to the MSWJR, No. 14, in 1895.

Soon after delivery, No. 16 gained the nickname 'Galloping Alice' possibly due to its strange rocking motion. At the grouping of 1923, the locomotive along with the MSWJR was absorbed into the Great Western Railway and was rebuilt with a standard boiler becoming its No. 24, acquiring a new nickname, 'Galloping Gertie'. Used on local freight duties around Swindon, it was withdrawn in 1930 and scrapped.

Much work has been undertaken to locate original

Midland & South Western Junction Railway No. 16, a new-build project for the Swindon & Cricklade Railway which runs over part of the company's main line. MSWJR

Oil painting of Claud Hamilton 4-4-0 No. 1790 at Felixstowe station around 1900.

drawings, with a significant number found in Australia and converted to CAD drawings for manufacturing use. Replicas of the maker's plates have also been cast at a local foundry in Cheltenham. However, the main thrust of activity in 2011 was to raise sufficient funds to build the main frames.

In May that year, another pre-Grouping new-build project was launched, to recreate a long-extinct class of Great Central Railway locomotive being recreated at an estimated cost of £500,000.

The chosen locomotive to replicate is No. 567, originally a Manchester, Sheffield & Lincolnshire Railway Class 2 4-4-0 which once hauled express trains across the Woodhead route.

A suitable cylinder block has been found and a GCR tender, the frames of which are suitable for reuse, has been obtained from the Midland Railway-Butterley and taken to the Great Central Railway (Nottingham) at Ruddington, while original Kitson drawings for the class have been located at the National Railway Museum.

The original No. 567 was one of a class of 31 locomotives built between 1887-94 at Kitson Works in Leeds and Gorton Works in Manchester. Popular and economical locomotives, they survived into the LNER era where they became Class D7. The last was taken out of service and scrapped in 1939.

The project, being undertaken under the banner of the 567 Group, could be completed inside a decade, it has been claimed. A decision has been made to opt for an all-new boiler rather than modify an existing one.

The new locomotive will be based on the modern-day Great Central at Loughborough, but will be available to visit other heritage lines.

Group chairman Andrew Horrocks-Taylor said: "These elegant 4-4-0s were the pride of the

MS&LR and then contributed towards the nascent GCR's slogan 'Rapid travel in luxury'. Indeed the GCR's legendary first chairman Sir Edward Watkin was so pleased with his Class 2, it was immortalised as the locomotive which features in the company crest.

"While we'll incorporate some minor changes, the new No. 567 will be externally indistinguishable from its predecessors."

The funding plan envisages 567 supporters signing up to give £5.67 a month for 10 years. Within days of the project launch at the GCR's spring steam gala, 50 supporters had signed up on this basis.

Finally, for now at least, a scheme to recreate one of the Great Eastern Railway's legendary D16/2 Claud Hamilton 4-4-0s has been launched.

It will be a replica of No. 8783, one of two Claud Hamiltons allocated to Royal Train duties. Although the original was unnamed, the new one will be called *Phoenix*.

It is intended that the locomotive will be used on heritage railways, although main line operation was also being considered.

The group certainly has the youngest officials of any new build scheme. The chairman, Christopher Allenby, at 20 one of the oldest, a mechanical engineering student at the University of Derby, is a volunteer at the North Norfolk and Ecclesbourne Valley railways. Treasurer Will Day, an engineering geology student at Portsmouth University, has a 93-years-old uncle who worked on the class when he was a steam driver at Cambridge.

The youngest official, assistant market researcher Timothy Clarke, is just 16. "While we are young we will use expertise when it comes to the engineering side of the build and for general guidance," said a statement on the group's website.

The first of the class, No 1900 *Claud Hamilton*, which appeared in 1900, was the largest and most powerful express locomotive on the GER, with 7ft driving wheels. It won a gold medal at the 1900 Paris Exhibition. A total of 117 survived to nationalisation, withdrawals beginning in 1955. No. 62613 was the last to be withdrawn, in September 1960 from March shed. None survived into preservation.

Associated with the new Claud Hamilton group is a scheme launched in 2011 by four teenage enthusiasts to recreate an LNER J39 freight 0-6-0, which first appeared in 1925, the last one of a class of 289 rendered extinct by the end of 1962. The group believes that the project will take 12-16 years, costing an estimated £1.2-£1.5 million to complete. The group's first step was to obtain a list of plans from the National Railway Museum and public meetings were being arranged to muster support.

Well, sceptics once said that *Tornado* would never happen!

J39 0-6-0 No. 2962, built at Darlington in 1931.

CHAPTER TWENTY SEVEN

A NEW MAIN LINE HERITAGE DIESEL?

WE HAVE SEEN PLANS AND PROJECTS to build new steam locomotives, both for use on the national network and at heritage railways big and small.

However, what are the chances of anyone recreating a classic standard gauge diesel locomotive to fill in the missing gaps in modern traction heritage?

When British Railways announced its Modernisation Plan in 1955, it sparked off a scramble both amongst the nationalised operator's regions and those of private manufacturers to produce diesel and electric locomotives to replace the steam fleet. Many superb types were designed and built, examples

Original 'Baby Deltic' D5900 at Hornsey, date unknown, probably on delivery from Vulcan Foundry via Doncaster Works. The photographer was the first depot manager at Finsbury Park. T GREAVES

of which are still in regular main line service today. Others were not as successful, or were produced on a localised basis and were unsuitable for use over the whole network. Some of these first generation types did not even see the end of British Railways main line steam haulage on 11 August 1968. Dai Woodham, the effective saviour of so many steam locomotives, cut up the last examples of two types of Western Region diesel hydraulics, North British Warship A1A-A1A D601 *Ark Royal* and Class 21 Bo-Bo D6122 at Barry in 1980 because nobody wanted them.

The main thrust and predominant image of railway preservation has always been steam, and this is why support has been forthcoming for new-build steam projects. The preservation of diesel and electric locomotives, once hated by enthusiasts because they replaced much-loved steam types with what was often seen as soulless boxes on wheels, took off much later, and while it has built up a very devout and widespread following, it is still a minority interest in the sector as a whole.

Back in the nineties, there was talk about building a new Class 21, and also recreating the experimental locomotive Birmingham Railway Carriage & Wagon Company's prototype Co-Co Lion, by tracking down one of the original engines and back converting a bodyshell from a Class 47, neither scheme bore fruit.

The problem of main line diesel new-build would be primarily one of finance. With modern traction having far less public appeal than steam, would sufficient numbers of people be prepared to contribute to what would be a very expensive project which in theory would include the machining of two new engines, a chassis and bogies, well into seven figures at best?

However, in September 2010, a highly affordable project to authentically recreate a lost British

Railways diesel class was launched at Barrow Hill roundhouse.

The Baby Deltic Project formally launched its scheme to create a replica of an English Electric Type 2. The group, which had successfully restarted the power unit from the last 'Baby Deltic' to be scrapped, announced its intention to convert a Class 37, No. 37372, into a modern-day example of a Class 23, in a project supported by the National Railway Museum, the Transport Trust, the Napier Power Heritage Trust, and the Rolls-Royce Heritage Trust. No. 37372 had been purchased from the Harry Needle Railroad Company in 2009 and would have been otherwise scrapped, so the project does not mean the loss of another locomotive from the heritage sector.

The project involves the shortening of the nose and body length of No. 37372, the restyling of the body and its mounting on Class 20 bogies so as to reproduce, so far as reasonably practicable, the appearance of a Class 23.

The bogies have been acquired already while the sole remaining Napier T9-29 engine, purchased from the National Railway Museum, has been rebuilt from a seized solid hulk to an operational unit by members over the last two and a half years.

It is hoped to create the new 'Baby Deltic' for as little as £30,000. The conversion will be undertaken at the Deltic Preservation Society's depot at Barrow Hill where the project will maintain a display.

British Railway's ten Bo-Bo Baby Deltics, numbered D5900-D5909, were built by English Electric in 1959. The Napier Deltic T9-29 nine-cylinder 1100bhp engine drove an EE generator, which powered the four traction motors. It was a half-sized version of those used in the more powerful Deltics which had ousted the great LNER Pacifics from the East Coast Main Line. That, coupled with their shorter body, led to the nickname 'Baby Deltic.'

The type entered service between April and June 1959 and were based at Hornsey, being used on King's Cross outer suburban duties such as the 'Cambridge Buffet Express' as well as services from King's Cross to Moorgate. They were later banned from Moorgate because of excessive exhaust smoke in the tunnels.

BR's National Traction Plan of the late 1960s aimed to standardise types of diesel locomotives in traffic, and led to the withdrawal of many of the classes that had been hastily introduced followed the Modernisation Plan of 1956 in order to oust steam as quickly as possibly.

Having suffered from operational problems, needing them to be re-engined, and the fact that there were only ten, meant that the Baby Deltics were a prime candidate for early withdrawal.

They were withdrawn between 1968-71, the last two being D5905 and D5909.

D5901 was transferred to the departmental fleet of the Railway Technical Centre in 1969.

It worked test trains to and from the centre until 1975, when it was replaced by a Class 24, and was finally cut up in 1977.

Opposite: A twenty-first century 'Baby Deltic' starts to take shape: Class 37 No 37372 with the sole surviving Class 23 engine running inside it. RJ SENIOR

APPENDIX
SO YOU WANT TO LIFT A SPANNER TOO?

All new-build groups are always on the lookout for fresh faces, whether it be volunteers, members or sponsors. Here are key contact addresses:

A1 *Tornado* and new Gresley P2 projects: Visit www.a1steam.com or write to: The A1 Steam Locomotive Trust, Darlington Locomotive Works, Hopetown Lane, Darlington, DL3 6RQ, email enquiries@a1steam.com

Baby Deltic: The Baby Deltic Project, Black Dub, Twyford, Barrow on Trent, DE73 7GA, email info@thebabydelticproject.co.uk or visit www.thebabydelticproject.co.uk

Beamish Museum: Visit www.beamish.org.uk or email museum@beamish.org.uk or tel: 0191 370 4000

B17s: visit www.nbloco.net or write to: NBL Preservation Group, B17 project, 4 Porchfield Close, Earley, Reading, Berkshire, RG6 5YZ.

BR Standard 2MT tank:
Visit www.bluebellrailway.co.uk/bluebell/locos/84030.html or email tony@tonyrail.fsnet.co.uk

BR Standard 3MT tank: Contact the 82045 Steam Locomotive Trust at Woodford, School Bank, Norley, Frodsham, Cheshire, WA6 8JY, telephone 01928 787255, email chris.proudfoot045@btinternet.com or visit 82045.org.uk

Brighton Atlantic Project: Contact Terry Cole at tcole@steyning.fsbusiness.co.uk
Great Western Society – new Saint, County 4-6-0 and 4-4-0, steam railmotor, 47XX – Richard Croucher, Great Western Society, Didcot Railway Centre, Didcot, Oxfordshire, OX11 7NJ, tel: 01235 817200 or mail info@didcotrailwaycentre.org.uk

Clan Pacific *Hengist*: Visit www. 72010-hengist.org or email info@72010-hengist.org or write to chairman John Drew, 15, Holburn Gardens, Ryton, Tyne and Wear, NE40 3DZ

Corris Falcon: Visit www.corris.co.uk or write to Peter Guest, 38 Underwood Close, Callow Hill, Redditch, B97 5YS

Ffestiniog and Welsh Highland Railways: Visit www.ffestiniograilway.org.uk or www.whrsoc.org.uk or tel: 01766 516035 or email tricia.doyle@festrail.co.uk

GER Claud Hamilton: http://claudhamiltongroup.webs.com/contactus.htm

GER F5: Visit the Holden F5 Locomotive Trust website at www.holdenf5.co.uk or email info@holdenf5.co.uk

Grange: The 6880 Betton Grange (Society) Ltd, 14 Newborough Road, Shirley, Solihull, West Midlands, B90 2HA, or visit www.6880.co.uk

Hunslet Engine Company: Visit www.hunsletengine.com

LMS Patriot No. 45551 *The Unknown Warrior*:
Visit www.lms-patriot.org.uk or write to The LMS-Patriot Company Ltd, PO Box 3118, Hixon, Stafford, ST16 9JL, email lms-patriot@hotmail.co.uk or tel: 07977 019051

Lynton & Barnstaple Baldwin 2-4-2T *Lyn*: Visit www.762club.com or write to Jon Pain at 26 Oaklands, Bideford, North Devon EX39 3HW

Manchester, Sheffield & Lincolnshire Class 2 4-4-0:
Email gcr567loco@yahoo.co.uk

Midland & South Western Junction Railway 'Galloping Gertie':
Visit www.swindon-cricklade-railway.org or tel: 01793 771615, email scr@gmx.co.uk

Moors Valley Railway: www.moorsvalleyrailway.co.uk

NER G5: Visit www.wrlpg.com or telephone Dave Foxton on 01388 817907 (evenings) or write to Weardale Railway Locomotive Preservation Group, 64 South Street, Spennymoor, County Durham, DL16 7TX

P2 Mikado: Nick Davison, 9 Hall Villa Lane, Toll Bar, Doncaster, South Yorkshire DN5 0LG, email enquiries@streamlinep2.co.uk

Southwold Railway *Blyth* project: www.southwoldrailway.co.uk or call 01502 724340